IMPLEMENTING AI SYSTEMS

TRANSFORM YOUR BUSINESS IN 6 STEPS

Tom Taulli

Apress®

Implementing AI Systems: Transform Your Business in 6 Steps

Tom Taulli
Monrovia, CA, USA

ISBN-13 (pbk): 978-1-4842-6384-6   ISBN-13 (electronic): 978-1-4842-6385-3
https://doi.org/10.1007/978-1-4842-6385-3

Managing Director, Apress Media LLC: Welmoed Spahr
Acquisitions Editor: Natalie Pao
Development Editor: James Markham
Coordinating Editor: Jessica Vakili

Distributed to the book trade worldwide by Springer Science+Business Media New York, 1 NY Plaza, New York, NY 10014. Phone 1-800-SPRINGER, fax (201) 348-4505, e-mail orders-ny@ springer-sbm.com, or visit www.springeronline.com. Apress Media, LLC is a California LLC and the sole member (owner) is Springer Science + Business Media Finance Inc (SSBM Finance Inc). SSBM Finance Inc is a **Delaware** corporation.

For information on translations, please e-mail booktranslations@springernature.com; for reprint, paperback, or audio rights, please e-mail bookpermissions@springernature.com.

Apress titles may be purchased in bulk for academic, corporate, or promotional use. eBook versions and licenses are also available for most titles. For more information, reference our Print and eBook Bulk Sales web page at www.apress.com/bulk-sales.

Any source code or other supplementary material referenced by the author in this book is available to readers on GitHub via the book's product page, located at www.apress.com/ 978-1-4842-6384-6. For more detailed information, please visit www.apress.com/ source-code.

Printed on acid-free paper

Contents

About the Author

Tom Taulli has been developing software since the 1980s. In college, he started his first company, which focused on the development of e-learning systems. He created other companies as well, including Hypermart.net, which was sold to InfoSpace in 1996. Along the way, Tom has written columns for online publications such as BusinessWeek.com, TechWeb.com, and Bloomberg.com. He also writes posts on artificial intelligence for Forbes.com and is the adviser to various companies in the space. You can reach Tom on Twitter (@ttaulli) or through his website (www.Taulli.com) where he has an online course on AI.

Introduction

There's an old joke: What's the difference between machine learning and artificial intelligence? If it's written in Python, it's probably machine learning. If it's written in PowerPoint, it's probably AI.

In other words, when it comes to AI, there remains quite a bit of hype! But this is typical of any megatrend in technology. Yes, the marketing can quickly get out of hand.

But despite this, the fact remains that AI is very real—and powerful. It has seen breakthroughs, such as with computer vision and language recognition. Hey, millions of people routinely use sophisticated devices like Siri and Alexa.

Yet it is still incredibly difficult to build AI systems. After all, the technology requires large amounts of data and the outcomes are generally based on complex probabilities.

So in this book, we are going to take a structured look at how to put together successful AI projects. Moreover, to get value out of this book, you do not need a technical background. It is meant for anybody involved in the AI process.

The focus is on providing a real-world approach. As a writer for Forbes.com, I talk to many founders, CEOs, and executives who are building AI systems. Thus, in this book, you'll get the benefit of some of their lessons and best practices. You'll get insights on the inevitable gotchas. And there are many.

This book will start off with two chapters that cover the fundamentals of AI. Some of the topics include the history of the field; the pros and cons; the key drivers of the growth and innovation; and the core concepts like machine learning, deep learning, NLP (natural language processing), reinforcement learning, and so on.

Then the book has six chapters that each cover a particular part of the AI creation process. Here's a look:

- Chapter 3: This chapter provides a framework to identify areas that will have the best chance of success with an AI implementation. The chapter will include various case studies, such as from Intuit, Halliburton, and Cadence.

- Chapter 4: AI requires a strong team with varying skill-sets and backgrounds. In this chapter, we'll take a look at the key roles, such as data scientists, project managers, business analysts, and data engineers.

- Chapter 5: Data preparation may not be an exciting topic but it is absolutely critical. Many AI projects fail because of problems with this. In this chapter, we'll look at some of the strategies to improve the results.

- Chapter 6: This chapter will cover the key steps for building an effective algorithm. There will also be an analysis of the various AI platforms that help to streamline the process.

- Chapter 7: The deployment and monitoring parts of the AI process can be challenging. Getting adoption of AI can be difficult because of fear or distrust. There are also issues with the erosion of models. In this chapter, we will look at ways to minimize the risks.

- Chapter 8: This chapter will look at how to deal with bias in models. There is also a case study of how Microsoft has been able to successfully use responsible AI.

Next, there will be a chapter about the future of AI. There will be a review of some of the trends in AI, such as quantum computers, regulation, and 5G.

And finally, at the back of the book, you'll find a glossary of common AI terms.

Accompanying Material

Any updates will be provided on my site at www.Taulli.com.

Foreword

We are now deep into the era of artificial intelligence. The speed of its advance has been phenomenal, opening up a horizon of untold promise and productivity, guiding your business decisions in thrilling, disruptive new directions.

Having been given the honor of writing a foreword to this compelling book, I'll add a few of my own observations as to AI's direction for our specific industry, the service desk, which plays a vital role in business today. Amidst the current pandemic, the service desk has become even more pivotal.

When it comes to integrating AI into business, we are still at the outset, but are poised for major progress. Broadly speaking, today's industry is very manual, hand-crafting specialized AI solutions for specific use cases or functions.

That means every business is tasked to implement its own solutions and hire its own data scientists. AI has met this demand by providing basic competence, open-source libraries for AI and machine learning (ML) platforms for testing AI models, and more.

But I predict that this will not last. The trend is toward turnkey, out-of-the-box solutions because of their superior economy, practicality, ease of use, consistency, and reliability. AI is evolving to virtual assistant capabilities, with such functions as supervised guided flows, unsupervised AI, cognitive search, live agent handoff, and so on.

I foresee two approaches predominating in the future. The first is fully verticalized AI solutions with scalable platforms, for a Salesforce-like SaaS solution. The second is AI platforms that allow customers to build their own solutions.

The role of data scientists will shrink as organizations gain the ability to buy customized vertical AI solutions off the shelf. That's a positive because there are simply not enough data scientists—a finite and costly resource. The most sensible strategy is to work around them and develop a verticalized platform available to companies.

When it comes to the cloud vis-a-vis AI and ML, containerized solutions are forcing highly scalable and parallelizable AI. AI and ML are designed to "hyperscale" architectures; most algorithms will be unsupervised and will include inherent learning.

The industry today is highly supervised but it won't always be. Why? Unsupervised learning uses AI algorithms to identify patterns in data sets containing data points that are neither classified nor labeled. The algorithms are allowed to classify, label, and/or group the data points contained within data sets without external guidance. In other words, unsupervised learning lets the system identify patterns within data sets on its own, grouping unsorted information according to similarities and differences when no categories are provided. Today, industries require data sets—tomorrow, you will not need them.

This is significant because unsupervised learning accelerates implementation (and thus time-to-value) for the AI solution. From concept to fully operational becomes a journey of weeks or months rather than years.

All of this impacts users of the AI-driven service desk with its tickets, knowledge, requests, and solutions. AI algorithms will shift the focus in the enterprise: the user will become the primary focus and the core, with everything built around that user.

Right now, AI and ML are expanding across IT service management, initiating a revolution, delivering the "Alexa-like" service desk experience that users need, want—and expect. The consequences include elevating the CIO to the strategic position of delivering the customer experience.

The AI-driven service desk reflects in lower costs and operational gains— trimming MTTR (mean time to repair) and reducing the outlay for providing customer support. The ability to create and personalize messages and engineer intelligent virtual customer assistants, automate support and operations tasks, and relieve staff of repetitive manual chores are all benefits of true digital transformation.

Conversational AI breaks new ground for leveraging back-end RPA tools to apply AI and ML to service functions, all via a natural language dialog flow through the omnichannel. Conversational AI encompasses natural language processing (NLP) and natural language understanding (NLU), which comprehends context and inputs in the form of sentences in text or speech format— integral to natural language processing. NLU search translates into interactive experiences for users and the ability to deliver intuitive "human" responses to user knowledge requests. The ability to answer common questions and assist in complex problems incalculably accelerates the remediation of issues, and, again, lowers costs.

Today, chatbots are progressing to a true virtual assistant capability, able to guide interactions with users through a workflow via a chat interface. This vision informs my company, Aisera, to deliver the technology capable of advancing from unsupervised AI to enabling conversational flow including NLU search. A cognitive semantic engine addresses user requests and escalates to a human only when deemed necessary. Aisera's mission is to make this process seamless, holistic, and "off-the-shelf" cost-effective.

The benefit of having a roadmap for your AI journey is impossible to overstate. This book takes you through the steps of AI deployment and sets out the fundamental processes to realize a successful mission: identifying the challenges you face, forming your team, preparing your data, creating a model for deployment, and monitoring the results. The book includes an indispensable discussion of ethics, along with case studies of off-the-shelf implementations, sharing the excitement of accomplishing a transformative goal.

Muddu Sudhakar, the Co-Founder and CEO of Aisera.

The AI Landscape

Pros and cons of the technology

In mid-January 2020, Nike announced that it hired John Donahoe for the CEO post.[1] He already had a good understanding of the company because of his role on the board of directors for five years. But it's important to note that Donahoe's prior experience was in the tech industry, as CEO at companies like eBay, PayPal, and ServiceNow.

Nike's move was notable—and in keeping with the company's culture of innovation. For the most part, the hiring of Donahoe was a clear sign that traditional companies need to put digital strategies at the forefront. It's table stakes.

His tech chops proved quite useful early on. When the novel coronavirus hit China in early 2020, Donahoe took swift actions to transform Nike to manage through the disruption. Even though he had to shut down Nike's retail outlets, the acceleration of ecommerce capabilities offset much of the decline in sales.[2]

---

[1]https://news.nike.com/news/board-member-john-donahoe-will-succeed-mark-parker-as-president-and-ceo-in-2020-parker-to-become-executive-chairman

[2]www.wsj.com/articles/nikes-quarterly-sales-pressured-by-coronavirus-closures-in-china-11585084649

© Tom Taulli 2021

T. Taulli, *Implementing AI Systems*, https://doi.org/10.1007/978-1-4842-6385-3_1

In an interview with the *Wall Street Journal*, this is how he described his strategy: "I bring a pretty simple mind-set. It is to see things through the eyes of the consumer. When you're buying something, you aren't thinking digital or physical. You're thinking, I want to get what I want, where I want it, how I want it. Increasingly, that's a blended digital and physical experience. I believe that experience is the future. The winning companies of the future will bring immersive, blended, digital and physical experiences."[3]

But to create this type of experience for the consumer, there needs to be next-generation technology. And yes, this means making major investments in AI. So it should also be no surprise that it is the world's top companies like Nike that are making this a strategic priority.

So why is AI so powerful? What is really going on with this technology? Let's take a look.

The Burning Platform

On the company's earnings call in late April, ServiceNow CEO Bill McDermott said: "Around the world, we see that customers who are farthest along in their digital transformation are better equipped to manage this crisis. Companies lagging behind are realizing that they now have a burning platform. Accelerating digital transformation has become a business imperative."[4]

He noted that the expected spending on digital transformation, which include major applications of AI, would be $7 trillion for the next three years. It's really a mind-boggling number. But for the most part, companies really have no choice anymore. They must go digital in a big way.

McDermott's reference to the "burning platform" goes back to a famous memo from the former CEO of Nokia, Stephen Elop (written in early 2011). It's about a story of a worker on an oil rig who awoke because of an explosion. His awful choice was to either stay on board or jump 30 feet into ice waters.

For Nokia at the time, the company was facing something similar: There was the disruption of both Apple's iPhone and Google's Android. According to Elop: "The first iPhone shipped in 2007, and we still don't have a product that is close to their experience. Android came on the scene just over two years ago, and this week they took our leadership position in smartphone volumes. Unbelievable."[5]

---

[3]www.wsj.com/articles/meet-the-new-nike-boss-trading-tech-for-air-jordans-11581166802

[4]www.fool.com/earnings/call-transcripts/2020/04/30/service-now-now-q1-2020-earnings-call-transcript.aspx

[5]www.theguardian.com/technology/blog/2011/feb/09/nokia-burning-platform-memo-elop

While he did implement some major changes, they were nonetheless too late. Apple and Google were able to build global ecosystems, which had incredibly powerful barriers to entry.

Nokia would eventually exit the mobile phone business and transition to becoming a provider of networking equipment. During all this, the company's market value would go from over $100 billion to about $20 billion (by the way, in the story of the worker on the rig, he would survive).

But we have seen the Nokia scenario play out many times. There was Netflix's upending of Blockbuster, Amazon.com's takedown of Borders, and Apple's undoing of Kodak. The examples and case studies could go on and on.

So is it any wonder that many executives are, well, very worried? Of course not. In fact, things are likely to accelerate even more. And perhaps one of the biggest catalysts is actually the COVID-19 virus.

"Digital transformation is no longer a buzzword or a long-term strategy," said Vivek Ravisankar, who is the co-founder and CEO of HackerRank.[6] "It's about near-term survival. COVID-19 is accelerating transformations that might have otherwise taken decades. COVID-19 resembles a unique societal crisis, unlike anything we've experienced in a generation. I recently came across a very interesting article from Boston Consulting Group which says that when crises of this magnitude occur, they lead to attitudinal shifts. These shifts lead to three things: new policies, newer ways of working, and new consumer behaviors. It's critical for companies to look at the world with this new lens, given this new reality. We are already familiar with the maxim of every company is going to be a software company but this pandemic is going to accelerate that transition by 10x. Just think about it, every bank needs to have the finest mobile app now (fewer in-person interactions), every healthcare provider should have a video calling facility (Epic system just built a new video calling facility with Twilio), and so on. The idea of rethinking your company to be digital-first is going to get more and more critical."

The Benefits of AI

AI is an exciting technology—and it is still in the early stages. But of course, it has already led to major breakthroughs and has been a game changer for many companies. For example, if not for AI, Google would not have been able to scale its massive search engine, which allows for super quick and accurate results. The technology has also been critical in providing for monetization, allowing the company to disrupt the traditional ad industry.

---

[6]This is from the author's interview with Vivek Ravisankar on April 2, 2020.

But of course, when it comes to AI, it is much more than better approaches to automation. Let's take a look at some of the other key advantages to this technology:

Insights: The simple fact is that many data sets are just too large for humans to understand! But with AI, it's possible to use algorithms to find interesting patterns that can identify revenue opportunities or ways to cut costs.

Improved decision making: In Marc Benioff's book, *Trailblazer: The Power of Business as the Greatest Platform for Change*, he describes how he uses his company's AI platform, Einstein, for his bi-weekly executive meetings. He writes: "After my executives offer their opinions and predictions about different regions, products, and opportunities, I turn to the virtual Einstein on my phone to see what he thinks."

Kind of awkward? Perhaps at first. But this management approach has been a big help. It has provided a more objective and unemotional voice for the meetings.

Wide application: Unlike various other technologies, AI can be used for many categories, whether for the law, HR, marketing, finance, sales, and so on.

Predictions: Traditional forecasting techniques are often subpar. They may be too simplistic and not leverage enough data. But of course, AI can make a major difference. The technology can not only better predict sales and churn, but also provide for applications like predictive maintenance (this is where an AI system can detect when a device or machine may break down).

Productivity: AI can speed up processes, which means reacting quicker to customers or emerging problems. It also allows for more time for employees to devote to value-add activities. Why waste time on mundane tasks?

"In today's world, speed to answers is critical to any company, not just for customer support but also for improved processes and faster decision making," said Kevin Gidney, who is the co-founder of Seal Software.[7] "The company that isn't using machine learning will be at a significant disadvantage."

Keep in mind that research from the McKinsey Global Institute forecasts that the gap between those companies that adopt AI and those that do not will only continue to widen.[8] The research shows that the adopters may double their cash flows by 2030. As for the nonadopters? The prediction is that there will be a 20% decline.

Errors: True, AI is not error-free. But when there is a solid model in place that is based on quality data, the results should be fairly consistent. Besides, the system can work on a 24/7 basis.

---

[7]From the author's interview with Kevin Gidney on April 19, 2020.
[8]`www.alteryx.com/sites/default/files/2019-05/Predictive-Analytics-Made-Practical.pdf`

Risky activities: We can use AI for dangerous activities. This is often the case with physical robots, which can be used in mines, deep water areas, or even in war zones.

Or look at self-driving technologies. Even though there is yet to be truly autonomous cars, the systems have still been key in helping provide more safety, such as with hazard detection capabilities.

Scale: Customer service volumes can vary widely. But AI systems, like chatbots, can help with this. These technologies can be configured to handle typical use cases, which means that a company does not have to hire a large number of people in a short period of time.

Customers: They are getting more accustomed to using AI, such as with standout apps like Uber, Facebook, and Siri. This means that companies need to get even more serious about their digital transformation efforts.

"Every business must now conform to the simple and unforgiving mantra of 'get-online or lose your customers' because that's where your buyers are likely to be, and that means it's harder than ever to get close to your customers through traditional sales approaches," said Geoff Webb, who is the VP of Strategy at PROS.[9] "Instead, businesses must divine the digital tea leaves, looking for intent-to-purchase signals, cross-referencing with market analysis, and filtering through a highly granular understanding of customer preference."

Volume: Every year, there are thousands of medical research papers published, and it's impossible for anyone to read them all. It's even challenging to keep up with just the content in a narrow area of medicine. But this is not a problem for AI. Systems like IBM Watson can read huge amounts of medical literature and summarize the key points and insights— saving much time and effort.

Learning: So long as the models are effective and there is high quality data, the AI system should be able to get smarter and smarter.

Social good: AI can help improve society, as seen in a report from McKinsey & Co., which has 160 use cases.[10] They show how the technology can help with poverty, natural disasters, and improving education. For example, a nonprofit called the Rainforest Connection uses TensorFlow to create AI models to locate illegal logging. This is done by analyzing audio files. Or there is the case where academics were able to develop a neural network to identify, through the use of drones, poachers in Africa

---

[9]From the author's interview with Geoff Webb on March 25, 2020.
[10]www.mckinsey.com/featured-insights/artificial-intelligence/applying-artificial-intelligence-for-social-good

The Drawbacks of AI

It's true that AI is far from perfect. After all, the technology is generally based on using probabilities that are based on large data sets. Even if there are minor issues, the results can be way off.

So then, what are some of the main issues and problems with AI? Here are some to consider:

Performance: Good software not only needs solid developers but also testers. This is even more important for AI since this technology can be complex and sensitive to slight changes.

Data: This is the fuel for most AI models. The problem then? It's that quality data is hard to find. Besides, even if you have a good data set, you still need to clean it up, which can take a considerable amount of time.

Black box: Some AI models are so complex and intricate, such as for deep learning, that it is nearly impossible to understand the rationales for the outcomes. This could make it so that the technology is not usable in certain contexts, such as for medical research, because of regulatory requirements.

Bias: You know the old saying of "garbage in, garbage out" (GIGO). It's a cliché. But this does not detract from its wisdom, as the GIGO concept is spot-on with AI. For example, if your data set is narrowly focused, such as on a demographic or a certain geographic area, then the results can easily be inaccurate. In some cases, the results could be damaging, such as when the algorithms are biased. This may mean, for example, that classes of people are denied a loan based on discrimination.

"56% of executives in a PwC survey have said they would find it difficult to articulate the cause if their organization's AI system were to provide inaccurate or biased information," said Anand Rao, who is the Global AI Lead at PwC.[11] "Meanwhile, the same survey found that 39% of respondents with AI applied at scale were only 'somewhat' sure they would know how to stop their system if something went wrong."

Job losses: As AI gets more sophisticated, the technology will start to undertake human-type activities. This could ultimately result in job losses, which could mean social and economic disruption. We've already seen this happen in various manufacturing industries because of the automation of robots. It's true that several studies point out that AI may ultimately lead to more job opportunities. But even if this turns out to be the case, there will still likely be a transition period, as people will need to go through reskilling.

---

[11] The author's interview with Anand Rao on March 29, 2020.

> ▪ **Note** A study from Geneys shows that 52% of U.S. workers believe their jobs have not been affected by AI. But when asked about what the impact will be within five years, the percentage goes down to 29%.[12]

Creativity: AI can provide some interesting insights and there are algorithms that can create interesting content. But the technology is nowhere near replacing a person's ability to come up with great ideas or concepts.

Judgement and emotion: Simply put, there are many human qualities that are currently not replaceable with AI.

"In recruitment, for example, AI can help to match candidates with companies based on their resumes, but only a human being can use interpersonal skills to find the best cultural fit for your company," said Allie Kelly, who is the CMO of JazzHR.[13] "Hiring teams will always be essential in forming and developing candidate relationships based on complex emotions and niche skill sets rather than intelligent design."

Costs: AI can be expensive, in terms of the consulting, software tools, and hardware/infrastructure. Then there are the costs for hiring talent, such as experienced data scientists. Oh, and then there are the costs of maintaining and managing existing AI systems.

Security: The hacking of AI models is becoming a bigger threat. This could mean that a self-driving car could be hijacked or turned into an autonomous weapon. Actually, with the enterprise, there could be intrusions on critical processes, such as those that involve sensitive data sets.

Diversity: This is sorely lacking in the AI field. A research study from New York University calls it a "disaster."[14] Consider the following:

- Over 80% of AI professors are male.

- Only 15% of the AI researchers at Facebook are female It's 10% at Google.

- About 13% of AI CEOs in the US are women.[15]

- About 71% of the applicants for AI jobs in the US are males.[16]

---

[12]www.genesys.com/press?release=122787
[13]From the author's interview with Allie Kelly on April 10, 2020.
[14]www.theguardian.com/technology/2019/apr/16/artificial-intelligence-lack-diversity-new-york-university-study?linkId=66248341

With a lack of diversity, there is more risk that the models will have bias or be inaccurate. There will also be challenges in getting better insights from data.

The Growth of AI

Sundar Pichai, who is the CEO of Alphabet, said this while at the World Economic Forum in Davos, Switzerland: "AI is one of the most profound things we're working on as humanity. It's more profound than fire or electricity."[17]

Granted, it got some blowback. Pichai's comment did seem to be over the top, even by Silicon Valley standards. Yet a big part of his job is to build cutting-edge AI that spans software and even hardware. So he is definitely someone to take seriously, right?

Absolutely.

When looking at just about any forecast or study about AI, the charts are upward sloping and involve substantial numbers. Take a report from International Data Corporation (IDC). It shows that spending on AI systems is expected to hit a whopping $97.9 billion by 2023, for a compound annual growth rate of 28.4%.

David Schubmehl, the research director of Cognitive/Artificial Intelligence Systems at IDC, said: "The use of artificial intelligence and machine learning (ML) is occurring in a wide range of solutions and applications from ERP and manufacturing software to content management, collaboration, and user productivity. Artificial intelligence and machine learning are top of mind for most organizations today, and IDC expects that AI will be the disrupting influence changing entire industries over the next decade."[18]

The report indicated that more than half of the spending came from banking, manufacturing, healthcare, retail, and professional services. But there was emerging growth in government, media, telecommunications, and personal/

---

[15]www.h2o.ai/democratizing-ai/
[16]www.theguardian.com/technology/2019/apr/16/artificial-intelligence-lack-diversity-new-york-university-study?linkId=66248341
[17]www.bloomberg.com/news/articles/2020-01-22/google-ceo-thinks-ai-is-more-profound-than-fire
[18]www.idc.com/getdoc.jsp?containerId=prUS45481219

consumer services. Just some of the common use cases included automated human resources (HR) and pharmaceutical research and development (R&D).

To get a sense of the growth in the AI industry, here are some other interesting studies:

- Accenture predicts that AI will double annual economic growth rates by 2035. The report also states that the technology will "[spawn] a new relationship between man and machine. The impact of AI technologies on business is projected to boost labor productivity by up to 40 percent by fundamentally changing the way work is done and reinforcing the role of people to drive growth in business."[19]

- Tractica, a technology research firm, forecasts that the AI software market will hit $126 billion in revenues by 2025.[20] While it's been mostly consumer tech companies that have thrived, the next phase will be growth in AI-based enterprise software companies.

- The number of peer-reviewed AI research papers shot up over 300% from 1998 to 2018.[21] In fact, China's output was about at the levels of Europe and exceeded the US. Countries like Singapore, Switzerland, Australia, Israel, the Netherlands, and Luxembourg have also been prolific (on a per-capita basis).

What Is Driving AI?

The tech world is famous for its buzzwords. They will initially gin up lots of excitement and venture capital investment. But then there will come a reality check—that is, the technology will often fall well short of the expectations. It's all too common.

But as for AI, the category has remained quite durable. Then again, as you've already seen in this chapter, the technology offers clear-cut advantages. Yet there are also some notable catalysts that have helped to fuel the growth.

---

[19]https://newsroom.accenture.com/news/artificial-intelligence-poised-to-double-annual-economic-growth-rate-in-12-developed-economies-and-boost-labor-productivity-by-up-to-40-percent-by-2035-according-to-new-research-by-accenture.htm?_ga=2.95939733.882226627.1588554804-1278195360.1586745913

[20]https://tractica.omdia.com/newsroom/press-releases/artificial-intelligence-software-market-to-reach-126-0-billion-in-annual-worldwide-revenue-by-2025/

[21]http://ide.mit.edu/news-blog/news/2019-ai-report-tracks-profound-growth

Here's a look:

- *Data explosion*: The emergence of mobile platforms, social networks, and cloud computing has resulted in enormous volumes of data. But there is also the Internet of Things (IoT), which uses sensors to collect huge amounts of data. With all this data, it has become much easier to create powerful AI models.

- *Venture capital*: Investors have continued to write checks to fund AI startups. During the first quarter of 2020, VCs invested in 285 startups in the sector in the U.S. for a total of $6.9 billion. But large tech companies like Google, Facebook, Apple, and Microsoft have also been making their own investments. Some of the rounds have been blockbusters. In July 2019, Microsoft announced a $1 billion round for OpenAI, which included a partnership with the Azure cloud platform. CEO Satya Nadella had this to say about the deal: "AI is one of the most transformative technologies of our time and has the potential to help solve many of our world's most pressing challenges."[22]

- *Deep learning*: During the past decade, there have been major breakthroughs with the theoretical aspects of AI. A key part of this has been the emergence of deep learning. This involves highly sophisticated models that can find patterns in huge amounts of data. The technology has been groundbreaking for applications like image recognition and self-driving vehicles.

- *GPU (graphics processing unit)*: In the early 1990s, Nvidia pioneered this semiconductor. Unlike a typical CPU (central processing unit), a GPU has a large number of cores that can handle thousands of threads simultaneously. At first, this technology was quite useful for high-end gaming platforms. But during the past decade, the GPU has also become a standard for handling the huge processing needs for AI models, especially with deep learning applications.

---

[22]https://news.microsoft.com/2019/07/22/openai-forms-exclusive-computing-partnership-with-microsoft-to-build-new-azure-ai-supercomputing-technologies/

https://venturebeat.com/2020/04/14/ai-startups-raised-6-9-billion-in-q1-2020-a-record-setting-pace-before-coronavirus/

- *Open source software*: This is software that is created by a community of developers. The technology is freely available, so long as any enhancement is provided for free. Because of this, open source software has seen significant growth. It's also been critical for the development of AI. There are a myriad tools and platforms like Python, Scikit-learn, Keras, TensorFlow, KNIME, PyTorch, Caffe, and Teano.

- *Mega tech operators*: These companies have not only been major investors in AI but also have been aggressive in hiring talent, such as from the world's top universities. Keep in mind that the mega tech operators are generally the source of much of the academic papers for AI.

How AI Can Go Off the Rails

AI has the potential for doing great harm to a company. Misuse of data or bad applications of models can damage the brand and loyalty of the customers. There may even be fines from government authorities.

Some of the world's top technology companies have been warning investors about such risks through disclosures to the Securities and Exchange Commission. Here's an example from Microsoft's 10-K annual report: "AI algorithms may be flawed. Datasets may be insufficient or contain biased information. Inappropriate or controversial data practices by Microsoft or others could impair the acceptance of AI solutions. These deficiencies could undermine the decisions, predictions, or analysis AI applications produce, subjecting us to competitive harm, legal liability, and brand or reputational harm. Some AI scenarios present ethical issues. If we enable or offer AI solutions that are controversial because of their impact on human rights, privacy, employment, or other social issues, we may experience brand or reputational harm."[23]

Granted, when it comes to corporate matters, the lawyers tend to be extra cautious. Might as well be prepared for the worse, huh?

This is true. But AI can certainly go off the rails. Interestingly enough, Microsoft has real-world experience with this.

Just look at the situation with its chatbot, Tay. This technology would actually go on to be a poster child of how bad AI can be!

---

[23]www.theverge.com/2019/2/11/18220050/google-microsoft-ai-brand-damage-investors-10-k-filing

The origins of Tay go back to 2014, when Microsoft implemented a chatbot on Tencent's WeChat social network in China. It turned out to be popular, attracting tens of millions of users.

Microsoft then wanted to bring the chatbot to the US. The company renamed it to Tay and put it on Twitter in March 2016.

Unfortunately, it was an absolute disaster. Tay suddenly started to repeat sexists and racist comments, primarily because the underlying technology was partly based on parroting messaging from users! Microsoft took down the app within 24 hours.

The company's corporate vice president of healthcare, Peter Lee, wrote in a blog: "Looking ahead, we face some difficult—and yet exciting—research challenges in AI design. AI systems feed off of both positive and negative interactions with people. In that sense, the challenges are just as much social as they are technical. We will do everything possible to limit technical exploits but also know we cannot fully predict all possible human interactive misuses without learning from mistakes. To do AI right, one needs to iterate with many people and often in public forums. We must enter each one with great caution and ultimately learn and improve, step by step, and to do this without offending people in the process. We will remain steadfast in our efforts to learn from this and other experiences as we work toward contributing to an Internet that represents the best, not the worst, of humanity."[24]

But AI can also have the potential to harm people physically. We got a terrible example of this back in March 2018, when an Uber self-driving vehicle hit a woman pedestrian and killed her.[25] There was a human driver, but the car was in the autonomous mode.

The National Transportation Safety Board investigated the matter for more than a year.[26] The conclusion was that Uber lacked sufficient safety and monitoring measures, as the driver spent a considerable amount of time checking his smartphone. The report also criticized state and federal regulators.

What about the technology? The report also showed that it was not adequately coded to handle pedestrians crossing streets when not in the crosswalks.

---

[24]https://blogs.microsoft.com/blog/2016/03/25/learning-tays-introduction/
[25]www.theverge.com/2018/3/28/17174636/uber-self-driving-crash-fatal-arizona-update
[26]www.theverge.com/2019/11/19/20972584/uber-fault-self-driving-crash-ntsb-probable-cause

Attitudes About AI

Back in 2009, Google's Sergey Brin saw the huge potential for self-driving cars and committed his company to being a major innovator in the category. He recruited Sebastian Thrun, the former director of the Stanford Artificial Intelligence Laboratory, to head up the effort. Consider that he led the team from Stanford that won the 2005 DARPA Grand Challenge for self-driving cars.

Google's investment would eventually turn into a division called Waymo. Yet the progress of the technology has not been swift. Along the way, Google has had to create its own sensors and other hardware. There has also been the need for intensive AI engineering to deal with the nuances of highways. For example, it has been difficult to get enough data. This is why Google has used 10 billion simulated miles for its AI models.

According to Waymo CEO John Krafcik: "Autonomy always will have some constraints. It's really, really hard. You don't know what you don't know until you're actually in there and trying to do things."[27]

But technology is not the only challenge. Waymo has had to deal with skepticism from the public. The fact is that many people simply are not confident with AI, at least for activities like driving. What's more, there are nagging concerns that the technology will result in lost jobs.

In a report in the *New York Times*, Waymo's self-driving cars in Chandler, Arizona, actually became an object of scorn and anger. Some people would throw rocks at the vehicles, point guns at them, slash the tires, and attempt to run them off the road.[28]

This may sound like an outlier but it really is not. As AI becomes more pervasive, there will be growing worries from the public.

Take an extensive survey of about 6,000 adults from Pegasystems, a top software company. When asked about their attitudes towards businesses using AI, the results were mixed. About 35% were comfortable with the technology but 28% were not.

The report concludes: "But some harbor deep-rooted fears about AI, and most still prefer the familiarity of the human touch over a faceless machine when given the option. For others, the AI experience isn't yet living up to their expectations. And across the board, we found most consumers just don't understand AI—not realizing how it already touches their lives every day."[29]

---

[27]www.cnet.com/news/alphabet-google-waymo-ceo-john-krafcik-autonomous-cars-wont-ever-be-able-to-drive-in-all-conditions/
[28]www.nytimes.com/2018/12/31/us/waymo-self-driving-cars-arizona-attacks.html
[29]www.ciosummits.com/what-consumers-really-think-about-ai.pdf

In other words, companies really need to be mindful of the sentiments toward AI. This means there needs to be ongoing education and training. It's also important to provide support, such as with reskilling of the workforce. If not, a company will likely not get the full benefits from AI.

■ **Note**   A study from Oracle and Future Workplace shows that 70% of employees use AI in their everyday personal lives but only 24% use it at their workplace.[30]

The Rise of AI-Driven Companies

In the book *Competing in the Age of AI: Strategy and Leadership When Algorithms and Networks Run the World*, Harvard professors Marco Iansiti and Karim R. Lakhani set forth an interesting vision of the future. It's about how there will be the emergence of AI-driven companies, which will redefine the norms of business. The competitive advantages will primarily be data, algorithms, and hyperscale. As the authors note: "[AI] is transforming the very nature of companies—how they operate and how they compete. When a business is driven by AI, software instructions and algorithms make up the critical path in the way the firm delivers value."

A company's future competitor may not be a traditional rival, either. It could be a startup that raises huge amounts of venture capital or a mega tech firm like Apple, Amazon, or Microsoft. Actually, Amazon has already demonstrated this multiple times, as the company has moved aggressively into categories like healthcare, advertising, package delivery, small business lending, video streaming, and cloud computing. It seems the only way to combat this giant is actually through antitrust laws since the market power is so dominant.

So then what does an AI-driven company really look like? According to Iansiti and Lakhani, the analogy is to think of an AI factory and it has four components:

- *Data pipeline*: There is a system that efficiently processes large amounts of data, such as by cleaning it, making sure there is compliance and detection for bias.

- *Algorithm development*: When approaching a problem, you want to use algorithms on data to find solutions. They essentially help make predictions. Some can be relatively straightforward, such as forecasting churn rates. But then you can get quite advanced, say with building a chatbot to interact with your customers.

---

[30]www.oracle.com/us/products/applications/oracle-ai-at-work-report-5037501.pdf

- *Experimental platform*: You want a system where it is easy to try out different ideas. For example, suppose you want to know the key factors for churn. The experimental platform should be the key.

- *Software infrastructure*: There needs to be a modern technology layer that relies on modular and component-based architectures. This makes it easier to evolve the AI as the technology gets more sophisticated.

All this takes time and investment to build. But it is well worth the effort. And once in place, there needs to be a culture that involves looking at all parts of the business with AI in mind.

To get a case study of this, take a look at Netflix, which was launched in 1997. The company's founders, Marc Randolph and Reed Hastings, had impressive tech backgrounds. But they brought more than just software abilities to Netflix. There was also a focus on using data to make better decisions. They used creative approaches to do this. In 2006, Netflix announced a $1 million (US) prize to anyone who could create a better algorithm for recommending films. The company open sourced a data set to help with the effort. As a result, the contest stirred up much interest and PR, leading to innovations in analytics. The $1 million turned out to be negligible compared to the benefits.

Being an AI-driven company, Netflix has become the global leader in streaming video, with a whopping 183 million subscribers.[31] The company's market value of $200 billion is actually higher than Disney's and Comcast's.

It seems that just about every part of the company's business is based on AI and analytics. For example, Netflix has teams of data scientists who research ways to improve the quality and speed of streaming. In some parts of the world, the Internet infrastructure is simply not robust but sophisticated algorithms can help deal with this, such as with optimal timing of caching.

But AI has also been extremely helpful in creating engaging content. According to Ted Sarandos, the Chief Content Officer at Netflix: "There's no such thing as a 'Netflix show.' That as a mind-set gets people narrowed. Our brand is personalization."[32]

Effective personalization means that Netflix can keep getting subscription fees from its customers, which can then fuel more investment in infrastructure, content, and AI. It's a virtuous cycle that has made the company highly competitive.

---

[31]www.wsj.com/articles/netflix-adds-16-million-new-subscribers-as-home-bound-consumers-stream-away-11587501078
[32]https://twitter.com/mip/status/1006084544758534144

Netflix built its own technology platform for the personalization, called Polynote. It works with other common AI tools like Apache Spark, Scala, and Python. In October 2019, Netflix open sourced the technology.[33]

Then what are the approaches to AI and personalization that Netflix uses? What has worked? Here are just a few:

AI thumbnails: Yes, a big part of the success of Netflix is the extensive content library. But this means little if users cannot find the show they want to watch. The irony is that people usually don't even know what they really like!

But AI has been critical in helping to solve this complex problem. Netflix processes huge amounts of data—in near real-time—on what is clicked, what is viewed and for how long, where there is rewinding, the device used, the time of day, and so on. The technology infrastructure has been built to track and measure every user interaction.

This approach to data is in stark contrast to the approach of the traditional Hollywood business model, which relies on demographic information like age and gender. But Netflix does not base its recommendations on this type of information. This kind of data simply does not have much predictive power.

As should be no surprise, the workflow of the Netflix system is quite structured. Here's a look:

- *Jump starting*: After you create an account or add a new profile, Netflix will ask you to choose some of your favorite titles. With this data, the system will begin to create your personalization graph. What if this step is skipped? Netflix will provide a diverse set of popular titles and iterate from this to get a better understanding of the user.

- *Supersede*: When you start watching movies on the service, the AI engine will negate the initial preferences. Also, the more recent titles will have more weight in the algorithms.

- *Ordering*: This matters. That is, the way titles are organized on the screen can help with improving the user experience. For example, a row has three layers of personalization: the choice of the row, which titles appear, and the rankings of how they appear. The strongest recommendations start from the top left and go to the right (unless the service is in Arabic or Hebrew).

---

[33]https://venturebeat.com/2019/10/23/netflix-open-sources-polynote-to-simplify-data-science-and-machine-learning-workflows/

This creates a continuous cycle of improvement. According to the Netflix website: "Our data, algorithms, and computation systems continue to feed into each other to produce fresh recommendations to provide you with a product that brings you joy."[34]

But the level of the personalization extends even to the artwork and photos of the thumbnails for each of the titles. The AI system will scan through the frames of each of the films and create a custom visual that is engaging. Often this is a picture of a popular actor. The AI models indicate that close-ups are usually better.

Back in 2014, Netflix's global manager of creative services noted that the thumbnail was the most important influencer on a user's decision about what show or movie to watch and accounted for more than 82% of the focus when browsing.[35] And timing was crucial. A user spent an average of 1.8 seconds when evaluating a title.

Test, test, test: This is a mantra at Netflix. You cannot assume something is true unless you have first tested the hypothesis with data and algorithms. For example, like many other sites, Netflix had user reviews. Sounds like a good thing, right?

Not at all. The data scientists tested them and the models showed that viewership went down because of the negative reviews!

Microgenres: Genre is fairly simple for traditional Hollywood films, with categories like Horror, Action, Suspense, Romance, Comedy, and so on. But for Netflix, this was not enough. The company set out to take a data-driven approach to create microgenres that are personalized to unique tastes (there are over 27,000).[36] Some examples include "Cult Comedies Featuring a Strong Female Lead" and "Classic Suspenseful Conspiracy Movies from the 1970s." By doing this, the AI engine could better match a movie to the user.

But interestingly enough, the creation of this data was not completely automated with an AI model. Netflix hired screenwriters and film fans to help come up with the microgenres. The main reason is that the company realized that AI really could not accurately determine microgenres by analyzing the film.

This is important since data-driven approaches can sometimes be counterproductive. Netflix has learned this the hard way with its experiences in Hollywood. When it uses thumbnails and other personalization techniques, there is sometimes anger from actors who feel they are getting ignored.[37]

---

[34]https://help.netflix.com/en/node/100639
[35]https://becominghuman.ai/how-netflix-uses-ai-and-machine-learning-a087614630fe
[36]www.finder.com/netflix/genre-list
[37]www.wsj.com/articles/at-netflix-who-wins-when-its-hollywood-vs-the-algorithm-1541826015

Or, in some cases, they may have projects that are very personal to them but may not necessarily get high viewership. Yet if Netflix wants to have long-term relationships with these actors, then there may be circumstance when it is best to ignore the data. It's a balancing act.

Search: This is an area that is crucial for the personalization experience. To get the best results, Netflix employs a variety of AI techniques like natural language processing, traditional machine learning, and text analytics. All this is built for many languages and cultural differences.

Marketing and messaging: To keep users coming back, Netflix uses email marketing and notifications. All are personalized based on user behavior. According to the Netflix website: "We deliver billions of messages per year, and we work on the personalization algorithms that decide what to send, when, and to whom. Our algorithm aims to optimize for member joy while being mindful of the volume of messages we send out." This extends to marketing campaigns on platforms like Facebook and Twitter, which are highly programmatic.

Creative: Of course, the Hollywood way for coming up with ideas is to rely on creative geniuses like Steven Spielberg and George Lucas. True, AI is nowhere near matching this ability but Netflix is using the technology to help supplement the process. This is vitally important for the company since it spends billions of dollars on original content.

So how does AI help out? Essentially, it makes it so that employees do not have to spend too much of their time on tasks like scheduling, budgeting, finding locations, handling post-production activities (to help with editing, sound, color correction, etc.), and localizing for different countries. The AI models optimize the costs along with the creative vision. To put things into perspective, scheduling a TV show or movie could easily take over 100 hours. Or consider post-production. In the case of the epic movie *Apocalypse Now*, the process took two years.[38]

The Challenges of AI

By reading stories in the media or hearing pitches for software companies, the perception is that AI is not necessarily difficult. But the reality is something different. When it comes to utilizing your company's data, finding use cases, building models and deploying them, there are many tough challenges. Now it's true that things are getting easier and the tools more powerful. But it will take some time until we get true "out of the box" AI.

---

[38]https://netflixtechblog.com/studio-production-data-science-646ee2cc21a1

Thus, if you are having troubles with your own efforts, do not despair. Many other companies do too—even companies that have strong technical teams and experience with software.

Here's a look at some of the surveys and research on the topic:

- In a survey from Accenture of 1,100 executives across the world, about 45% say they have deployed sustainable AI systems that are creating acceptable benefits.[39]

- Research from Pactera Technologies estimates that 85% of AI projects do not meet planned business benefits.[40] One of the main reasons is the lack of senior management support.

- A survey from IDC shows that, for those organizations that use AI, only about 25% of them have the technology deployed on an enterprise-wide basis.[41] The report also shows that the failure rate for projects is up to 50%. Just some of the reasons for this include issues with recruiting technical talent and unrealistic planning.

The Democratization of AI

The pace of development of AI tools and systems is staggering. This has allowed for lower costs, better capabilities, and improved ease of use. The bottom line: It's getting easier for just about any company to use AI.

"AI can benefit all companies and help smaller companies punch way above their weight class," said David Linthicum, who is the Chief Cloud Strategy Officer at Deloitte Consulting LLP.[42] "You can now utilize the technology to provide a better strategic advantage."

Udit Gupta, who is the former Head of Product at Zomato and a founder of an Y Combinator AI startup, agrees: "Anyone who says that AI is just for the larger companies is probably unlettered in the field. The technology for setting up AI and ML has been fairly commoditized, so anyone including individual developers, small companies, and late stage companies can deploy AI to their current projects fairly quickly. Tech giants like Amazon, Google, and Apple are all working to provide plug and play solutions for companies to integrate AI into their products."[43]

---

[39]www.accenture.com/_acnmedia/pdf-73/accenture-strategy-ai-momentum-mindset-exec-summary-pov.pdf
[40]www.techrepublic.com/article/why-85-of-ai-projects-fail/
[41]www.businesswire.com/news/home/20190708005039/en/
[42]From the author's interview with David Linthicum on March 25, 2020.
[43]From the author's interview with Udit Gupta on April 29, 2020.

Despite all this, there will still need to be a focus on training of the core concepts of AI and data analytics. The fact is that models require much critical thinking and understanding of statistics, probability, and data analysis.

Another interesting trend, in terms of the democratization of AI, is the emergence of the citizen data scientist. Gartner describes it as follows: "[This is a person who] creates or generates models that use advanced diagnostic analytics or predictive and prescriptive capabilities, but whose primary job function is outside the field of statistics and analytics. Citizen data scientists are 'power users' who can perform both simple and moderately sophisticated analytical tasks that would previously have required more expertise. Today, citizen data scientists provide a complementary role to expert data scientists. They do not replace the experts, as they do not have the specific, advanced data science expertise to do so. But they certainly bring their OWN expertise and unique skills to the process."[44]

By having citizen data scientists, you are creating a more data-driven organization and getting more value from AI efforts. But this will also help with the challenges in recruiting, as many large companies have been aggressive in luring trained data scientists. It really is tough to compete in this environment.

But cultivating citizen data scientists in an organization requires a major commitment in terms of ongoing training. This could mean online courses or even college instruction. With the training, these citizen data scientists may ultimately want to become data scientists, which would mean even more career advancement.

The Hardware Factor

The main focus of this book is on software-based AI. Why so? When it comes to the enterprise, the key way people develop and interact with this technology is through using tools, algorithms, and data. Besides, when it comes to hardware, such as AI chips, they are often for those with specialized backgrounds within an organization, or these technologies may be accessed via the cloud.

Yet this is not to minimize the importance of this part of AI. Hardware systems are crucial for the development and growth of AI. What's interesting is that many of the top players in this category are companies known for their software prowess like Microsoft, Facebook, Google, Baidu, and Alibaba. These companies realize that they need a holistic approach to investing in next-generation AI.

---

[44]https://blogs.gartner.com/carlie-idoine/2018/05/13/citizen-data-scientists-and-why-they-matter/

As noted earlier in this chapter, GPUs are the most common for data crunching and modelling. By using more cores on the chip, they can greatly speed up the process of running experiments or delivering AI in real time.

Now while GPUs are certainly powerful, there are certainly limitations as well. One of the big issues is with deep learning, which requires constantly changing the weights of the neurons. This can slow down the training process when using a GPU. But there are other issues like energy consumption, the communication between cores, and the challenges with matrices. Oh, and GPUs are not cheap!

Because of all this, some of the world's top AI experts believe that more needs to be done with hardware systems. For example, this was a major topic of discussion when Geoffrey Hinton, Yann LeCun of Facebook, and Yoshua Bengio joined for a press conference at the MILA Institute for AI in late 2019.[45]

Despite this, there are hopeful signs. Here are just some examples of the innovation with AI chips:

- *Tensor Processing Unit (TPU)*: Google announced this chip in the summer of 2016 at its I/O conference, although the company had been using this technology for its AI applications for at least a year before. As the name implies, the TPU is built specifically for Google's TensorFlow deep learning platform and is meant for scale. For example, a chip can process 100 million photos a day.

- *Habana Goya Chip*: Intel acquired Habana for $2 billion in late 2019 because the company's own AI chip, the Nervana neural network, was not as good in terms of compute power.[46] Another advantage was that the Habana chip had a large customer base. Note that back in 2016 Intel acquired Nervana Systems for about $350 million. In other words, the AI chip space does move quickly and cutting-edge technologies can quickly fade away.

- *Neuromorphic chips*: These chips are designed similar to human brain cells or neurons. This technique can be quite effective for deep learning and other neural networks. Intel has been experimenting with neuromorphic chips, such as its Pohoiki Beach system, which can simulate up to eight million neurons.

---

[45]www.zdnet.com/article/ai-on-steroids-much-bigger-neural-nets-to-come-with-new-hardware-say-bengio-hinton-lecun/
[46]https://siliconangle.com/2020/02/02/intel-dumps-nervana-neural-network-processors-habanas-ai-chips/

- *Huge chips*: Yes, these are semiconductors with enormous numbers of transistors. One example is from startup Cerebras Systems, whose AI chips have a whopping 1.2 trillion transistors.[47] This not only greatly increases processing rates but is generally more energy efficient. However, there is a nagging problem: the size. It's about as large as an iPad so it may be too big for certain applications.

Conclusion

The AI field is certainly exciting and dynamic. In this chapter, we have only scratched the surface of the many aspects of the market.

While AI is challenging and requires focus, the process is getting easier. And this trend will only continue. This definitely bodes well for the success of the technology for many companies.

As for the next chapter, we will cover some of the fundamentals of AI.

Key Takeaways

- The growth in AI is forecasted to be strong for the long haul. A report from IDC predicts that spending will reach $97.9 billion by 2023, for a compound annual growth rate of 28.4%.

- Digital transformation is becoming a must-have for many companies. A critical part of this is the adoption of AI.

- Some of the benefits of AI include lower costs, more revenue opportunities, better insights through analyzing data, higher productivity, lower error rates, and the scaling of services.

- Some of the drawbacks of AI include challenges with implementation and building models, data quality and access, bias, lack of human-style judgment and creativity, costs, security vulnerabilities, little diversity, and even potential job losses.

---

[47]https://venturebeat.com/2019/09/21/the-ai-arms-race-spawns-new-hardware-architectures/

- The past decade has seen great strides in the development of AI. Some of the drivers include the explosion of data, such as from social networks, cloud computing platforms, and IoT; growth in venture capital investment; breakthroughs in deep learning; the use of GPU chips; the growth in open source AI platforms; and the impact of mega AI operators like Google, Microsoft, and Facebook.

- There is emerging a new type of modern company that is driven by AI, like Netflix. Many of the decisions and systems are based on data analysis. AI companies have the potential for being highly competitive and disruptive.

- AI is still a challenge and takes a major commitment. The fact is that many projects still fail.

- But AI technology is getting more democratized. The power is increasing in terms of the features and the pricing is reasonable.

- While this book is focused on software-based AI, this is not to minimize the importance of hardware. AI chips are essential for the growth of the industry. Note that there has been more innovation in the space, such as with next-generation technologies like neuromorphic chips.

AI Foundations

What can the technology really do?

The pace of innovation with AI is stunning. Take a look at a study from Northwestern Medicine, which involved a collaboration with Google AI. The project used over 42,000 CT lung scans from more than 14,000 patients to train an AI model (the process only took about ten minutes). The bottom line: The model did better than a radiologist when detecting cancer and there was a 11% reduction in false positives.[1]

Here's what Shravya Shetty, Google's AI leader on the project, had to say: "This area of research is incredibly important, as lung cancer has the highest rate of mortality among all cancers, and there are many challenges in the way of broad adoption of lung cancer screening. Our work examines ways AI can be used to improve the accuracy and optimize the screening process, in ways that could help with the implementation of screening programs."[2]

But of course, AI has its dark sides. It can be the source of discrimination when the underlying data is biased or violates privacy, such as with facial recognition.

Keep in mind that, for many years, there have been vigorous debates about the benefits and dangers of AI. And this will likely remain the case as the technology continues to grow and become more pervasive.

---

[1]https://thinkml.ai/top-5-ai-achievements-of-2019/
[2]https://dailynorthwestern.com/2019/05/22/lateststories/northwestern-medicine-and-google-use-ai-to-improve-lung-cancer-detection/

© Tom Taulli 2021
T. Taulli, *Implementing AI Systems*, https://doi.org/10.1007/978-1-4842-6385-3_2

In 2019, Tesla CEO Elon Musk and Alibaba cofounder Jack Ma had a wide-ranging discussion about AI, showing how stark the opinions can be.[3] Ma took a mostly optimistic tone, saying: "I think AI is going to open a new chapter of the society of the world that people try to understand ourselves better, rather than the outside world. ... And I don't think artificial intelligence is a threat. I don't think artificial intelligence is something terrible, but human beings are smart enough to learn that."

As for Musk, his view was more dour. He noted: "Well, computers actually are already much smarter than people on so many dimensions. We just keep moving the goalposts. ... Hopeless, we are hopeless. Hopelessly inadequate. In terms of rendering into—basically there's just a smaller and smaller corner of what of intellectual pursuits that humans are better than computers. And that every year, it gets smaller and smaller, and soon will be far surpassed in every single way. Guaranteed. Or civilization will end. Those are the two possibilities."

So in light of all this, is it any wonder that AI can be confusing? Definitely not.

In this chapter, we'll look at the roots of AI, the different approaches, and some of the use cases.

A Brief History of AI

It comes as a surprise to many people that AI has been around for decades. As you will see later in this chapter, it was brilliant mathematicians, like Alan Turing, who started to theorize about this technology during the 1930s—even before computers existed.

But when it comes to a concrete time period when AI became a serious endeavor, this was during 1956 at Dartmouth University. John McCarthy organized a ten-week seminar called "Cerebral Mechanisms in Behavior." It was for this event that he coined the phrase "artificial intelligence." The funny thing is that this term was met with mostly criticism yet no one could come up with something better.

The conference included professors who would ultimately go on to become pioneers in the AI field, including Marvin Minsky, Oliver Selfridge, Ray Solomonoff, Claude Shannon, Julian Bigelow, Allen Newell, and Herbert Simon. Some of the topics covered were natural language processing, neural networks, and abstraction.

But the most notable part of the seminar came from Newell, Cliff Shaw, and Simon, who provided a demo of the world's first AI program: the Logic Theorist. The idea for this came while Simon worked at the Research and

---

[3]www.wired.com/story/elon-musk-humanity-biological-boot-loader-ai/

Development (RAND) Corporation, which is where he saw computers print words on a map for the purpose of air defense against a potential first strike from the Russians. This showed that these machines were much more than just calculators. They could handle images, characters, and symbols, which could lead to insights—even help save the world. As for the Logic Theorist, it was able to solve 38 of the first 52 theorems in Chapter 2 of the *Principia Mathematica*.[4] Keep in mind that the program solved one of them more elegantly than the book! And for this, the co-author, Bertrand Russell, wrote a note that showed he was quite impressed with the feat.

In those early days of the Computer Age, the development of programs was exceedingly difficult and tedious. The machines had little memory or computational power. The languages were also low-level and complex, which involved using punch cards with a series of 1s and 0s. As a result, Newell, Shaw, and Simon created their own language, called IPL or Information Processing Language, and came up with innovations like list processing (this was for dynamic allocation and deallocation of memory). So yes, the Logic Theorist was certainly a major achievement.

From 1956 to 1974, this era would often be considered the "Golden Age of AI." But interestingly enough, little of the financial support came from private industry (this was primarily due to the fear that there would be blame for lost jobs from automation). Rather, it was the US government that wrote many of the checks, which would go to institutions like Stanford, MIT, Lincoln Laboratories, and Carnegie Mellon University. The main reasons for this spending: the Space Race and the Cold War.

No doubt, there was much progress with the AI applications as computers got more sophisticated. Here are just some:

- *General Problem Solver*: This was another AI application from Newell, Shaw, and Simon. It could solve math problems like the Tower of Hanoi.

- *LISP*: McCarthy created this computer language in 1958, which would become the standard for AI development. The language also included concepts like recursion, dynamic typing, and garbage collection.

- *ANALOGY*: This was the mastermind of MIT professor Thomas Evans. The application was able to solve analogy problems from an IQ test.

---

[4]https://history-computer.com/ModernComputer/Software/LogicTheorist.html

- *STUDENT*: This was the result of the PhD thesis from MIT student Daniel Bobrow. With the help of Minsky, he developed one of the first natural language processing systems. The focus was on solving high school algebra problems.

- *ELIZA*: This is perhaps the most famous AI program from the 1960s (you can find live versions of it on the Internet). ELIZA was the first chatbot for the purposes of psychoanalysis. While the program was relatively simple—it generally would just repeat questions in a different form—there were people who thought it was a real person, which deeply concerned the program's creator, MIT professor Joseph Weizenbaum.

- *Computer vision*: This field got its start back in 1966! The story is that Minsky tasked a student to spend the summer finding ways to effectively link a camera to a computer and then have a program describe the views.

- *Mac Hack*: A popular use-case for AI was to create a program to play chess. But it was the Mac Hack that was able to play in tournaments, getting a C-rating.

In these formative years of AI, there were two emerging theories about AI. On one side, there were symbolic systems, whose main proponent was Minsky. This approach to AI was about creating logical if/then decision trees to codify knowledge.

Then there was the theory that looked to the human brain for guidance. At the core of this was something called the neural network or the perceptron. With this, algorithms would ingest data and then try to find patterns. The leader of this approach was Frank Rosenblatt, who was actually a psychology professor at Cornell. In 1957, he built a computer called the Mark I Perceptron that demonstrated the neural network. It had a camera that could compare two rudimentary images. With the algorithms, the computer would use random weights to optimize the results.

The computer did cause a stir and got a profile in the *New York Times*, which boasted that the technology would unleash thinking machines. Yet this would prove to be premature since the perceptron was quite basic, with only one layer.

It also did not help that Minsky wrote a book in 1969 called *Perceptrons* (the co-author was Seymour Paper) that aggressively attacked Rosenblatt's theories. And this was devastating, as researchers would ultimately avoid the theory.

Years later, Minsky would say his book was off the mark and that there was merit to neural networks. After all, this approach to AI would ultimately become known as deep learning.

By the early 1970s, though, AI would start to lose favor. It would become known as the AI Winter. And this would be the first of several that would occur in the next 30 years.

Why did AI lose steam after having so much momentum? Despite all the investments in AI, the results were mostly disappointing. The simple fact was that computer technology was not powerful enough to create useful applications, especially for the military or the Apollo space program. Hey, what was the need for something that could only understand some equations or play better chess?

Not a lot.

Even the LISP language was far from ideal. It just did not have the capability for high-end analysis.

In the meantime, the US economic boom was ending, as inflation and unemployment started to rise. The spike in oil prices only added to the problems. And of course, the Space program was starting to wind down and there was even some level of detente with the Russians.

But perhaps the biggest blow to the AI cause was a report published in 1973, which came from Professor Sir James Lighthill. The UK funded this effort and the conclusion was stark: the technology was overhyped. At the heart of this was the issue of how models quickly got too complicated and were not easy to adjust (this was known as "combinatorial explosion"). The report was even part of a BBC program, which did more damage to AI, especially with the general public.

Because of all this, the US government started to cut back on funding. The result was that researchers would instead look at other areas of computer science study.

However, AI would morph into other applications. This was evident in the trend of expert systems, which was spurred by corporate investments in mini-computers and PCs. These applications essentially codified the knowledge of top people in certain fields like medicine, finance, and manufacturing.

One of the most successful expert systems was developed by John McDermott at Carnegie Mellon University. His AI program was called XCON (eXpert CONfigurer) and it optimized the selection of computer components. Think of it as an early version of a recommendation engine, such as what you see on Amazon.com when you look up something to purchase. DEC adopted the XCON and sold it along with its highly popular VAX computer. Through the 1980s, this would be a big money maker for the company. If anything, it was one of the first successful commercial AI systems.

But there were some problems with the expert systems. They tended to be too narrow and did not scale effectively into other categories. What's more, as an expert system grew over time, the coding often got too complicated to maintain and this meant more errors.

Besides expert systems, there were other interesting AI innovations during the 1980s, despite the adverse impact of the AI Winters. For example, German Professor Ernst Dieter Dickmanns made a self-driving car in … 1986. This was done by placing cameras and sensors on a Mercedes-Benz van. With sophisticated software, it was possible to steer the vehicle and change the speed. When Dickmanns tested it on a highway, the car could hit a speed of 60 mph and had a fairly smooth ride. The AI system essentially focused on optimizing the processing of images, which was no easy feat because of the limited capabilities of computers at the time. Even with the success, though, Dickmanns was unable to get enough funding for his project.

But there were also key theoretical developments for AI during the 1980s. Professor Kunihiko Fukushima developed the Neocognitron, which could recognize patterns, and this became the foundation for convolutional neural networks. He looked at the visual cortex of animals to come up with this approach (this is the part of the brain that allows the eyes to work).

A few years later, Professor John Hopfield wrote a paper about a new AI system, which he called the Hopfield Networks. But the more common name was the recurrent neural network.

By the late 1980s, the AI community saw an acceleration of innovation. To this end, Professor Yann LeCun combined convolutional neural networks with backpropagation, which was used for analyzing handwritten pages. Then there was Christopher Watkins' PhD thesis entitled "Learning from Delayed Rewards," which was focused on reinforcement learning.

But the most pivotal breakthrough in AI theory came in 1986. Professors Geoffrey Hinton, David Rumelhart, and Ronald J. Williams published "Learning Representations by Back-propagating Errors." It was a game changer and became one of the most cited papers in AI. The conclusion was that backpropagation could be used to greatly improve the accuracy of models. It was also a vindication of Rosenblatt's beliefs about neural networks.

More and more, these innovations would become part of real-world software applications. Note that some of the main adopters of the technology were financial firms because they needed to find ways to help combat fraud and process loan applications more efficiently. But the search engine market was another major user of AI. Google, for example, used the technology to scale its fast-growing platform—not only for processing queries but to manage the complex ad transactions.

So by 2010, AI reached a key inflection point. With the computing power at more sufficient levels, it was now possible to create robust models. The general public got an illustration of this from the popular game show *Jeopardy!* IBM's Watson AI computer took on two champions—and beat them.

Here are some of the other notable events:

- *Siri (2011)*: Apple launched this personal digital assistant, which put AI in the hands of millions of people across the globe.

- *Image recognition (2012)*: Professors Jeff Dean and Andrew Ng published the results of an experiment that analyzed ten million unlabeled images from YouTube. The model was able to show a high degree of accuracy in recognizing cats.

- *More image recognition (2012)*: Professors Alex Krizhevsky, Ilya Sutskever, and Geoffrey Hinton published a groundbreaking paper titled "ImageNet Classification with Deep Convolutional Neural Networks." It illustrated how a convolutional neural network had an error rate of only 16% in recognizing photos in ImageNet.

- *Go (2016)*: Google's DeepMind unit created an AI system based on reinforcement learning that was able to beat the world's top Go player, Lee Sedo (four games to one). Keep in mind that the conventional wisdom was that AI would never be able to conquer this game because the possible positions were more than the number of atoms in the universe!

What Is Intelligence?

The Oxford dictionary defines intelligence as "the ability to learn, understand and think in a logical way about things…."[5]

But this is still vague since there are many aspects to intelligence. It involves highly complex systems like the brain, which can remember information, learn and understand concepts, use language, engage in logical thinking and problem solving, spin up creative ideas, and so on. According to Thomas Edison, "The chief function of the body is to carry the brain around."[6]

---

[5]www.oxfordlearnersdictionaries.com/us/definition/english/intelligence
[6]www.brainyquote.com/quotes/thomas_a_edison_149044?src=t_brain

In light of the fact that understanding intelligence is so difficult, how is it possible to determine if a computer can be intelligent? Well, interestingly enough, Alan Turing took this on in 1950 with his paper entitled "Computing Machinery and Intelligence." He was one of the world's top mathematicians and was considered one of the first computer scientists (he came up with some of the core concepts for programming in 1936, when he was in his early 20s).

In his landmark paper, he realized that coming up with a definition of intelligence was futile. But there was an interesting workaround: The Imitation Game, which would later be called the Turing Test.

It's essentially a thought experiment. There are three rooms. One has a computer and another a person. The third room contains a person who is a judge. He or she engages in a free-form discussion with the two participants. If it is not clear who the human is, then the Turing Test has been cracked—that is, the computer is intelligent.

Alan Turing actually thought this would ultimately happen in 2000 or so. But he was proven wrong. Over the years, there have been several contests, such as the Loebner Prize and the Turing Test Competition, to see if an AI system can win. But the judges have been able to identify the computer.

■ **Note** The Turing Test was even an inspiration for science fiction writers! One was Philip K. Dick, who read Turing's paper and used it as the basis for his Voight-Kampff test, which was for determining if someone was a human or a replicant (that is, an android). This was the heart of his novel, ***Do Androids Dream of Electric Sheep?***, and would then be used in the iconic movie ***Blade Runner***.

But in 2018, Alphabet CEO Sundar Pichai gave a demo that seemed to show that the Turing Test was finally defeated. This was at the I/O conference and he used Google Assistant to call a local hairdresser to make an appointment. And it worked!

However, there was a problem: the conversation was not open ended. It was focused primarily on a certain task.

There are definitely many critics of the Turing Test, though. One of the biggest arguments against it is that an AI system can essentially be tricked, such as by using certain twists with sentences or intentionally making errors.

But Alan Turing was aware of the weaknesses with this theory and did address them. One was actually based on concepts from Ada Lovelace, who lived during the 1800s. She worked with Charles Babbage to create mechanical computers. Lovelace believed that a computer could not do anything that was already programed. In other words, it would not be creative like a human being. And so far, this has turned out to be the case.

So how did Turing address this? Well, interestingly enough, he posited that perhaps there really wasn't anything really new! Granted, this was not necessarily a good argument.

Despite this, the Turing Test is still looked to as a framework for thinking about AI.

Strong AI and Weak AI

In 1980, philosopher John Searle published a paper that got quite a bit of attention: "Minds, Brains, and Programs." He took on the Turing Test by creating his own, which was called the Chinese Room Argument. This was his thought experiment: Suppose Jane is in a room and she does not speak Chinese but she does have a translation book. In another room is John, who does speak Chinese. Under the door, he passes messages in the language and Jane then uses the translation book for the answers. Basically, John thinks he is talking to someone who understands the language.

So what's the takeaway with this thought experiment? Searle believed that what Jane was doing was no different in what a computer would do. That is, instructions were being carried out in a mechanical way. More importantly, this meant that there was really no thinking. Let's face it, Jane does not understand Chinese, right?

Yes, it's a very good argument against the Turing test. But Searle would go even further. He would set forth the two main parts of AI:

- *Strong AI (this is also known as artificial general intelligence or AGI)*: This is when the technology truly understands reality. This is where AI becomes what we see in the movies, such as with *Star Wars*.

- *Weak AI (or narrow AI)*: This is software that is focused on a narrow area like optimizing a company's supply chain or determining anomalies for fraud detection.

There are a handful of companies that are investing in Strong AI like Google's DeepMind as well as OpenAI. But these organizations are not focused on commercialization of their technologies, at least in the near term. The goal is to push the boundaries of AI in a big way.

OK, So What Really Is AI?

This is a tough question to answer! Even experts have their own definitions. It does not help that the media and many entrepreneurs provide their own concepts of what AI is as well.

Given all this, it's understandable why the topic engenders so much confusion. Yet I think there is a way to get an understanding of AI—that is, to use a visual. So take a look at Figure 2-1.

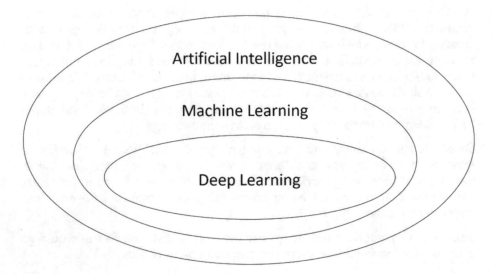

Figure 2-1. This is a high-level look at the key components of the AI world

AI is the complete topic of machine-based intelligence, which includes both strong and weak versions. Then there are various subsets like machine learning, deep learning, and natural language processing. Each have their own types of algorithms and use cases.

So in the rest of this chapter, we will cover these subsets.

Machine Learning

The roots of machine learning go back to the late 1950s. IBM researcher Arthur Samuel coined the term by saying it is the "field of study that gives computers the ability to learn without being explicitly programmed." True, this is another vague term. Then again, machine learning is a broad topic, so it is difficult to define.

"Machine Learning is a term that applies to algorithms which learn from data," said Alyssa Simpson Rochwerger, who is the VP of AI and Data Evangelist at Appen. "Generally speaking, it integrates perception, prediction, reasoning, and decision-making capabilities into one product or application."[7]

There are different types of machine learning, which include supervised learning, unsupervised learning, reinforcement learning, and semi-supervised learning. Let's take a look at each.

Supervised Learning

Supervised learning, which is the most common approach to machine learning, is when you have labeled data sets. For example, suppose you want to build a model to detect cats. This would mean that you have pairs in the data, as follows:

- *Subject*: This is the input value. It could, for example, be a photo of a cat.

- *Supervisory signal*: Yes, this is the output value. In our example, the label would simply be "cat."

A machine learning algorithm will attempt to find patterns in the data. This is done by continuously tuning weights for the equations.

An advantage of supervised learning is that it is much easier to assess the accuracy, since there is an output value to compare against. To accomplish this, there is a loss function, which measures the error rate. In fact, it's called "supervised learning" because it is like when a teacher evaluates a student's answers.

But there are some nagging issues with this approach:

- You generally need large amounts of data to have a model that effectively learns. It could be in the millions or billions or more.

- Much of the available data in the world is not labeled. And if you want to create labels, this can be a time-consuming process.

- Supervised learning cannot be used in real time. The reason? Well, there is the need to create the labels, after all.

- There is usually a need for lots of computation to train the models.

---

[7]From the author's interview with Alyssa Simpson Rochwerger on May 25, 2020.

Supervised learning has two main flavors. First of all, there is classification. As the name implies, this is when an output value is within a certain category. An example of this is your spam filter for your email inbox. The classification algorithm has two outputs: spam or not spam. Thus, there will be ongoing training to see what emails fall within each of the categories.

Next, there is regression. This is where the output value is continuous, such as a dollar amount or weight.

For both classification and regression, there are a myriad of algorithms to choose from. We will next look at some of them:

- *Regression*: Linear and multiple regression analysis
- *Classification*: Logistic regression, support vector machines, random forest, K-nearest neighbor, and Naïve Bayes classifiers

Regression Analysis

The roots of regression analysis go way back to the early 1800s. The pioneers were mathematicians like Adrien-Marie Legendre and Johann Carl Friedrich Gauss. At first, the use case was for predicting the orbits of comets around the sun.

Yet regression analysis would prove quite versatile. Keep in mind that this technique is widely used in academic papers across many disciplines but also in corporations, such as for forecasting.

So how does regression work? To see, let's first go over a simple version of regression: linear regression.

Here's the equation:

$$Y = c + bX + error$$

Y is the dependent variable or the output of the model. It's the value that we want to predict. The X variable, on the other hand, is the independent variable. This is what we put into the equation to get the prediction.

Then there is the b variable, called the coefficient, that quantities the relationship between Y and X. This is based on analyzing the patterns in a data set and finding the "best fit line." Regression measures the errors of each of the data items and quantifies those that have the least errors.

As for the c variable, it is the constant. This means that Y will have a value even if X is zero. The c variable is also based on analyzing patterns in a data set.

OK then, let's see an example of a linear regression. Suppose you want to predict sales for your product. To do this, you create a data set for the marketing expenditures for the past five years. You then use a software system like Excel or a set of Python packages or R to compute the regression formula (this uses such techniques as calculus and linear algebra), which is

$$Y = 5 + 1.5X$$

Assume this is in thousands. So if you spend no money on marketing, you will get $5,000 in sales. This could be the result of word-of-mouth or more sales from existing customers.

But if you spend $25,000 on marketing, your sales will hit $42,500. Figure 2-2 shows the graph of this regression.

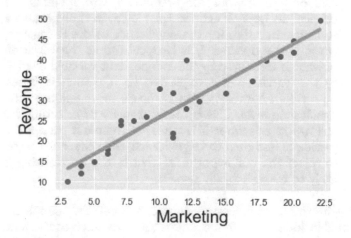

Figure 2-2. This is a graph of a regression line for predicting revenues based on the amount of marketing expenditures

This plots the marketing expenditures and the revenues for your data set. The orange line is the estimated line. But of course, there is variation. Marketing is not the only factor when predicting revenues.

Although, by looking at the chart, you can see that there appears to be a strong relationship between marketing expenditures and revenues. But there are a myriad of metrics you can use to measure the accuracy.

Here are some examples:

- *Standard error*: This shows the variation for the constant and the independent variable. You want a low number for this. As for your model, the constant has a standard error of 1.873 and the dependent variable has a value of 0.149.

- *R-squared*: This is how much a regression equation explains the output. In our example, the R-squared is 0.871—that is, the marketing expenditures account for 87.1% of the prediction for the revenues. Then what is a good R-squared? There are no bright lines. For example, with an area like physics or chemistry, an R-squared of 0.70 or better might be pretty good. But a value of 0.20 or better would be acceptable with subjects like political analysis or economics. However, there is also a statistical measure for the significance of the R-squared, which is the p-value. This is calculated as the variation of what is explained by the independent variable divided by the variation not explained by it, which is based on random data sets. You compare the p-value to the significance level. This is the probability of rejecting the null hypothesis when it is true. For the most part, if the p-value is less than the significance, then there is reason to reject the null hypothesis. That is, the relationship is likely to be statistically significant.

OK then, with the sales forecast example, it is certainly simplistic. A better model would include other independent variables, such as the amount spent on the sales force, the pricing, and perhaps even the weather conditions. When you have more than one variable, then you use a multiple regression formula. While it is fairly similar to a simple one, there are some important differences. For example, a regression line is not calculated. The reason is that the chart will have more than two dimensions. The focus instead is to compare the accuracy of one model to the next. For the most part, you will be trying out different independent variables to get a sense of which ones have the most explainability.

To do this, you will use the adjusted R-squared, which is modified for the number of independent variables. You can also look at the p-values.

Something else: You do not want to have too many independent variables. This will likely give a false sense of the overall accuracy. Instead, the goal is to have several key variables that have the most statistical significance.

Note So what's the difference between an algorithm and a model? Both words are often used interchangeably. Yet there are important differences. An algorithm is one or more general equations. A simple one is for linear regression: $y = c + bx$. A model, on the other hand, is when the equation has values for the parameters. To use our example, this is $y = 3.4 + 1.2X$.

Logistic Regression

So far, you've seen how regression analysis can be used to help make predictions, assuming the data is fairly linear. But what if this assumption does not apply?

Or, suppose you want to create a model that helps a business person make a decision. Example: If you increase the price of a product by 20%, how many customers will be lost?

To help with such use cases, you can try logistic regression analysis. It is for outcomes that are categorical or binary like "yes" or "no" or "1" or "0."

Let's then take an example for churn. We have a data set where we have different prices for the product and a value of 1 if there is churn and 0 if not. After computing this, we get Figure 2-3.

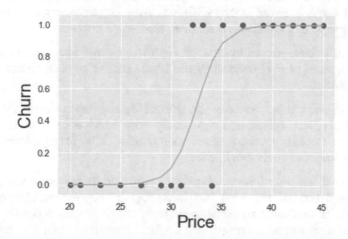

Figure 2-3. This is a graph of a logistic regression equation to predict the churn rate based on the change of the price of a product

Yes, it's a non-linear line that is shaped like an "S" and the bounds go from 0 to 1 (the name "logistic" comes from the type of function used to create this type of curve). Based on this, if the price goes from $20 to $25 or so, there is zero chance of churn. But after this, the odds of churn start to increase until it is $37 or so, at which there is a 100% probability churn.

Compared to regression analysis, there are differences with logistic regression when evaluating the statistical significance of the model. There is a metric called log-likelihood, which is almost always negative—and the bigger the number, the better. There is also the LLR p-value, which is similar to the p-value for regression analysis. You want this to be close to zero.

What about R-squared? There are different versions here as well. For example, there is the McFadden R-squared, which indicates that a model is good if it has a score of 0.20 to 0.40.

Then there is the confusion matrix, which is a simple chart that has four values that show the predictions compared to the actuals. Here's an example in Figure 2-4.

	Predicted: 0	Predicted: 1
Actual: 0	7.0	1.0
Actual:1	1.0	11.0

Figure 2-4. This confusion matrix shows the predictions for the logistic regression model

With this, you can see that for the prediction of churn, the model got this correct 11 times but was wrong with one. And for predicting no churn, there was also one wrong outcome but seven that were correct.

Using these values, you can come up with the overall accuracy, which is the number correct (11 + 7) divided by the total number of predictions (11 + 7 + 1 + 1) or 90%.

OK then, so what about some of the uses of logistic regression in the business world? To see, let's consider a case study from ServiceNow, which is one of the world's fastest growing cloud companies. The firm's platform helps customers improve their workflows.

Over the past few years, ServiceNow has retooled its software with machine learning, and one of the keys has been logistic regression algorithms. An example is its service management system, which routes incoming support tickets without human intervention. Logistic regression can find patterns in the data to optimize the workflows and decisions. For example, Novant Health has autoamted about 40% of self-service tickets because of ServiceNow. The model showed an accuracy rate of about 79%. Then there is the University of Maryland, whose system has 85% for auto-routing and a 4X faster average time to close a case.

"ServiceNow uses logistic regression as a classifier," said Debu Chatterjee, who is the Head of ML, AI, and Analytics Engineering at ServiceNow. "The classification capability is generic and can be leveraged to solve various use-cases. It is ServiceNow's experience that logistic regression provides a good model quality baseline that is generally difficult to beat. But there are other benefits like better scalability, model explainability, and good out-of-the-box probability output calibration. Good output calibration makes model fine-tuning easier for general users who are not data scientists."[8]

Support Vector Machines

A support vector machine is a classifier that uses a line called the optimal hyperplane that evenly separates different types of data. To get a sense of this, see Figure 2-5.

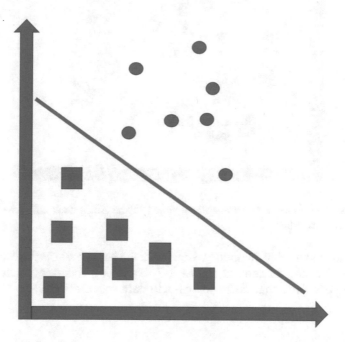

Figure 2-5. This shows the hyperplane line that separates data for a support vector machine

You can see that there are two types of data: one in the form of boxes and other as circles. The line between them shows the optimal hyperplane.

But if the data is not linear, then you can use the kernel method to transform the graph into more than two dimensions. This should better separate the data to allow for a hyperplane line.

---

[8]From the author's interview with Debu Chatterjee on May 29, 2020.

Let's take a look at an example. Suppose we have data like the following in Figure 2-6. As you can see, it is non-linear and overlaps. It would be impossible to compute a hyperplane line.

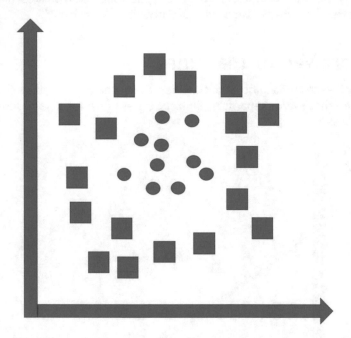

Figure 2-6. This shows a two-dimensional view of data, which does not allow for the creation of a hyperplane line

But now let's see what happens when we use the kernel method to make to make a 3-D chart, as seen in Figure 2-7. By taking this perspective, we can create a hyperplane that cuts through the data more effectively.

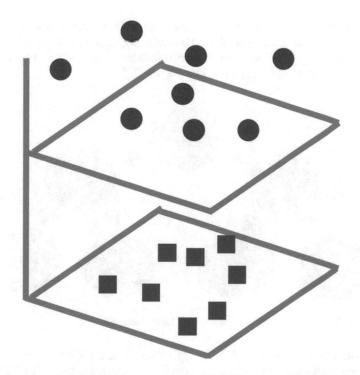

Figure 2-7. This shows a three-dimensional view of the data and a hyperplane line

Regarding the advantages of support vector machines, they are helpful when dealing with complex relationships. The main reason is that they can deal with non-linear relationships. There is also better handling with outliers since there is more emphasis on data that is closer to the hyperplane.

But support vector machines can take considerable compute power and there may be less transparency. If a model has a large number of dimensions, you will not be able to get a visualization.

Random Forest

For the most part, machine learning algorithms can be complicated and use sophisticated mathematics. But the random forest approach is much different. It's actually quite intuitive and easy to use. Yet this does not detract from the usefulness of the algorithm.

A random forest is a set of different independent decision trees. This is also known as an ensemble method because it uses several machine learning models in order to help improve the accuracy of the predictions.

To understand this, let's see an example. Suppose you have data from an ERP system for invoices and you want to understand the process. You take a sample of this data and have the random forest calculate the relationships in the form of decisions. It may look like Figure 2-8.

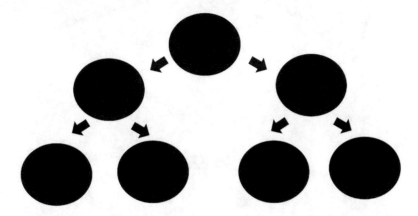

Figure 2-8. Here's a visualization of a random forest decision tree

When you use new data with the random forest model, it will generate predictions based on these decision trees. For example, with the ERP data, it might determine when an invoice will be paid automatically or when there will need to be approval from the finance department.

In general, the random forest algorithm works well using categorical and continuous data sets. It is also quick to create and relies on less compute power. However, when it comes to complex relationships, the random forest is not likely to be the right approach. And even though there is a visualization, it can still be hard to interpret if there are many decision trees.

K-Nearest Neighbor

The K-nearest neighbor algorithm is based on the assumption that similar data will be close to each other. It goes with the old saying: "Birds of a feather flock together."

There are several important advantages to the K-nearest neighbor algorithm. For example, it is non-parametric, which means there are no assumptions about the data. This is critical because other algorithms often have strict requirements.

Next, the K-nearest neighbor algorithm is fairly easy to work with and requires no training. Yet it is still able to make good predictions.

To use the algorithm, you need a data set that has known categories of data, such as for customer segments (small, medium, and large companies). Then you plot these groups on a 2D graph. Figure 2-9 shows an example with two types of data.

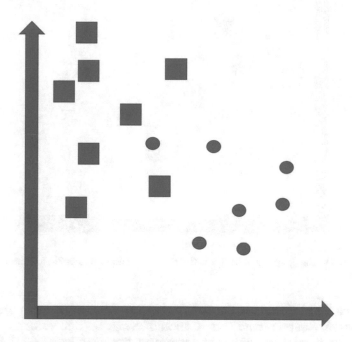

Figure 2-9. Here's a graph with two categories of data

You then place a new data point (which you do not know the type of) on the graph. Generally this will be in the middle of the items. This is noted as K on the graph, in Figure 2-10. You then set K to five, which means you draw a circle around the five nearest items.

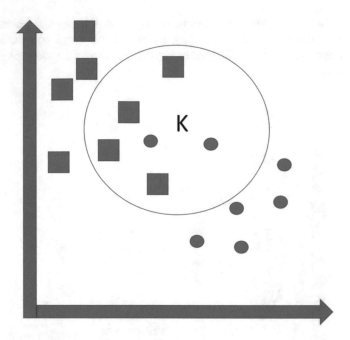

Figure 2-10. In this graph, you have set the K to five and have a circle for the nearest data items

Since there are more square data points than circle ones, you can predict that K is a square. Keep in mind that K should always be odd so as to avoid any ties. And the number should not be too large because there will likely be less accuracy.

This illustration of the K-nearest neighbor algorithm is certainly a simplistic model but it does show the basic concept. For example, there are a variety of approaches to find the proximity to the data items like Euclidean distance, hamming distance, and the Manhattan distance (which is actually based on the city block framework of the city!). These methods do involve some complicated equations, though.

Then what about the real-world use cases for the K-nearest neighbor algorithm? These include text mining, stock market analysis, and risk factors for certain diseases.

However, the K-nearest neighbor algorithm does have its drawbacks. Perhaps the biggest one is the arbitrariness of coming up with the placement and value of K. Variations can have a notable impact on the outcome of the model.

Naïve Bayes Classifiers

Naïve Bayes classifiers are based on the Bayes' theorem, which is a key part of calculating probabilities in traditional statistics. At a high level, it is about the odds of event A happening given event B, assuming that both events do not depend on each other (this is why it is called naïve).

Sounds kind of tricky? It can be. Yet the Naïve Bayes classifier is common in machine learning and has been shown to be quite effective.

In order to get a better understanding of this technique, consider an example: a spam detector. The first step is that there is email data that are labeled as either spam or not. Let's suppose that for the spam we have 10,000 words (you know, those that are over the top and have exclamation points!)

The next step is to read a new email and see if it contains one of the words on the spam list. With this, you then use the Naïve Bayes classifier to see the probability that an email with the word is spam.

True, it's straightforward. But it is useful since there is no need to deal with any dependencies between the two events. As a result, the analysis is much easier (in terms of the mathematics) and quicker.

Another benefit is that if the email has more than one of the words on the list, like "Viagra" and "Cialis," then the probability that it is spam will increase, which is what you want.

"It's truly remarkable: we make a silly simplification just to make the math easier, and it ends up actually performing better," said Noah Giansiracusa, who is an Assistant Professor at Bentley University. "One other great thing about the Naïve Bayes classifier is that it is what's called an 'incremental learner.' Most machine learning algorithms have to be retrained from scratch when you collect more training data, but not with Naïve Bayes. This is because it is just based on frequencies from word counts. As you collect more training data, you can just update these word counts and frequencies as you go. That's actually why it's important in your own email program to click 'mark as spam' or 'not spam' when you read your email. You are actually providing more labelled data to your spam filter as you do this, and since almost all spam filters are based on Naïve Bayes, they can instantly learn from this information and update the model."

Unsupervised Learning

Simply put, unsupervised learning is where the data is not labeled. Rather, algorithms attempt to infer patterns and structures, which are often not detected by the human eye because of the large volume of data. Since data is often messy and not labeled, unsupervised learning is critically important for successful machine learning.

As for the downsides, this type of machine learning can be extremely complex and requires much computing power. You generally need highly trained experts to properly train the models. Unsupervised learning is also not easy to measure and evaluate, such as in terms of the accuracy.

There are numerous approaches to consider for this type of machine learning:

- Clustering
- Anomaly detection
- Association
- Autoencoders

We'll now take a closer look at each of them.

Clustering

As the name implies, clustering is grouping similar data items. This is actually the most common technique for unsupervised learning.

Clustering is often confused with classification. But there is a major difference: yes, it's about the labeling of the data. With clustering, the algorithms try to detect patterns for the data points.

So how is the grouping done? For the most part, you need to come up with a similarity measure, which divides the data into different features. A simple example of this is different genres for books, like horror, adventure, science fiction, and so on. These features are put into clusters and each gets a cluster ID.

Next, you use different types of algorithms. What's more, they do not necessarily scale well when there are massive data sets.

So let's take a look at some of the algorithms for clustering:

Hierarchical-based clustering: This is where the data is organized in a tree structure. It is most appropriate for things like taxonomies. You can see an example of this in Figure 2-11.

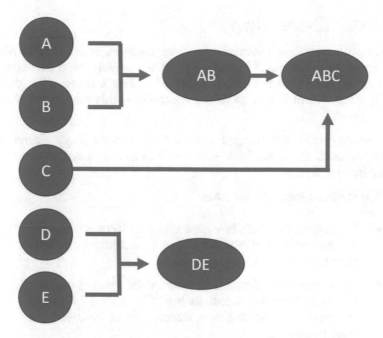

Figure 2-11. This graph provides an example of a hierarchical-based analysis

In this chart, you start with five data items (A, B, C, D, and E). You then iterate through them to find what is common. First, A and B are similar so they are grouped. This cluster then has commonalities with C. And yes, you group this to get ABC. As for D and E, you group them.

Centroid-based clustering: This relies on the K-means algorithm, which iterates through the data set to determine clusters that do not overlap. You first specify the number of clusters, which is denoted by K. Next, centroids are placed in the data set to get a sense of the distribution. This continues until there are no changes in the centroids.

However, as you learned earlier in the chapter with k-nearest neighbors, the use of centroid-based clustering is highly sensitive to where the initial data items are placed.

Density-based clustering: With this, an algorithm looks for areas where similar data items are concentrated but also surrounded by empty space or lightly populated data points. Any of the data that is not included in a cluster is assumed to be noise.

There are three main algorithms for density-based clustering: defined distance (DBSCAN), self-adjusting (HDBSCAN), and multi-scale (OPTICS).

Anomaly Detection

Anomaly detection is a method that uses machine learning algorithms to detect unusual data items. A common approach is with fraud detection, such as with credit card transactions. If a person makes a transaction that is far from the norm when it comes to prior activities, this may mean that there could be fraud.

But there are many other applications of the technology. Some include detecting tumors from an MRI scan or finding intrusions in a company's network infrastructure.

There are various types of anomalies:

- *Point anomalies*: This is where one data item is an outlier. An example is if an ecommerce transaction is much higher than those from the past.

- *Contextual anomalies*: This is unusual data that is based on the overall environment, such as the season or time of the week. For example, a transaction at 2:00 AM may raise concerns.

- *Collective anomalies*: This is when a group of data items are far outside the rest of the data set, although the data items within the group are consistent with each other.

An anomaly also does not have to mean something negative is happening. It could actually point to an emerging new trend. This could alert businesses to opportunities to sell products or services.

There are numerous approaches to detecting anomalies. They can be easy, say by using simple statistical measures like standard deviations. But of course, you can apply machine learning, such as regression analysis or k-nearest neighbors, to find the outliers, as well as advanced deep learning models.

A big challenge with anomaly detection, though, is the noise in the data. This may be just random changes that may look like outliers but are really not.

A case study of how to use anomaly detection is MindBridge, which uses AI for its audit system. Among its hundreds of accounting firm clients, one used the application to uncover a $2.8 million fraud committed by a controller of a company. This was based on the analysis of over six million transaction records.[9]

---

[9]www.forbes.com/sites/forbesfinancecouncil/2019/02/14/how-ai-could-protect-your-business-from-financial-fraud/#7f678e616116

Association

Association is about analyzing large non-numeric data sets to find certain rules. Think of it as using if/then statements. The process is quite fast but effective.

In fact, association is common with applications like recommendation engines. Keep in mind that the real power of this is when the machine learning system finds patterns that are not intuitive. For example, suppose Amazon analyzes huge amounts of data on people that buy books about AI. The data scientists then compare this to other transactions. Perhaps they realize that there is a high probability that such a person will also buy something like tea!

Regarding algorithms for association, a popular one is Apriori, which came about from a famous paper from R. Agrawal and R. Srikant in 1994. It is based on searching and testing the data set for frequent subsets and then adding them into groups. The algorithm ends when no additional rules are found.

While association can certainly be effective, there are issues with the approach. Consider that data often has different frequencies that may not necessarily mean anything or are just random. This can easily mean that the model will produce inaccurate results.

Autoencoders

A blog from Nvidia has a pretty good way of describing autoencoders: "Autoencoders take input data, compress it into a code, then try to recreate the input data from that summarized code. It's like starting with Moby Dick, creating a SparkNotes version, and then trying to rewrite the original story using only SparkNotes for reference."[10]

It seems kind of fanciful but a sophisticated neural network can be used to pull this off. But why would someone want to use something like an autoencoder?

The applications are not extensive, actually. But the algorithm has been shown to be useful in helping do things like clean up photos and videos. This can also help with self-driving cars and medical analysis, such as of X-rays. Autoencoders can even be effective with topic modelling, which allows for finding concepts and insights from large sets of documents.

---

[10]https://blogs.nvidia.com/blog/2018/08/02/supervised-unsupervised-learning/

Semi-Supervised Learning

You guessed it: semi-supervised learning is a blend of supervised and unsupervised learning! However, there is generally much more unlabeled data. Then by using sophisticated algorithms, such as deep learning approaches, it is possible to essentially create new data to fill the gaps. Next, you train the new data set and create a machine learning model.

But semi-supervised learning has some inherent drawbacks, especially with accuracy. There really is no way to have solid benchmarks to work from.

Despite this, semi-supervised learning has been a major area of focus for machine learning. Amazon CEO and founder Jeff Bezos mentioned this topic in his 2017 shareholder letter: "In the US, UK, and Germany, we've improved Alexa's spoken language understanding by more than 25% over the last 12 months through enhancements in Alexa's machine learning components and the use of semi-supervised learning techniques. (These semi-supervised learning techniques reduced the amount of labeled data needed to achieve the same accuracy improvement by 40 times!)"[11]

Or take a look at a case with Facebook. The company used its massive photo repository from Instagram to create new data sets by analyzing hashtags. Granted, there were some issues, such as with ones that were not descriptive (like #tbt or "throwback Thursday"). This is why researchers called the approach "weakly supervised data."

But the results were still pretty good, with the accuracy rate at 85.4% (this was based on the ImageNet recognition system). To pull this off, Facebook used 336 GPUs, which shortened the training process from a year to a few weeks. According to the company blog: "With ever-larger model sizes—the biggest in this research is a ResNeXt 101-32x48d with over 861 million parameters—such distributed training is increasingly important. In addition, we designed a method for removing duplicates to ensure we don't accidentally train our models on images that we want to evaluate them on, a problem that plagues similar research in this area."[12]

The emergence of GANs or generative adversarial networks is another cutting-edge area of machine learning that has bolstered semi-supervised learning. The mastermind of this is Ian Goodfellow, who got the idea while celebrating his friend's graduation from a PhD program. It took place at a popular bar in Montreal.[13]

---

[11]www.infoworld.com/article/3434618/semi-supervised-learning-explained.html

[12]https://engineering.fb.com/ml-applications/advancing-state-of-the-art-image-recognition-with-deep-learning-on-hashtags/

[13]www.technologyreview.com/2018/02/21/145289/the-ganfather-the-man-whos-given-machines-the-gift-of-imagination/

What did they talk about? Well, one of the topics was about whether an AI system could generate realistic photos. For the most part, deep learning models were far from effective with this task. As a result, making a new photo resulted in something strange like a nose in the wrong place! It was kind of like looking at a Picasso.

So yes, Goodfellow had a freewheeling conversation. But it really got him to think deeper about the topic. When he went home, he started to code some of his approaches to solve the problem. His inspiration: What if you could have two neural networks compete against each other? Might this be a better approach?

It certainly was. Thus was born the GAN. It was actually similar to the pioneering work in AI back in the 1950s when IBM researcher Arthur Samuel created a game to play checkers.

But of course, the GAN was much more sophisticated and based on some of the latest developments of deep learning. Actually, because of this, Goodfellow became one of the biggest names in the AI world. He went on to work at Google and then Apple. He also wrote a top book called *Deep Learning*.

A key advantage of a GAN is that it does not require much data. Rather, the system creates new data or synthetic data. What's more, since the GAN is constantly iterating, there is usually ongoing improvement in the accuracy of the predictions.

Something else: There is no need to have labeled data. This is because there is the inference of patterns in the underlying data.

Here's a high-level look at how this algorithm works. One network is called the generator and the other is the discriminator. First, the generator is built to create data. This could mean, for example, using part of a photo and random data to make a new image. Regarding the discriminator, it has multiple hidden layers but there are only two areas for input and the output is either 1 for a real image or 0 for a fake. If there is a fake, then it is returned to the algorithm through the process of backpropagation and there are changes to the weights. This process continues as new content is created.

Researchers have been able to use GANs for a myriad of purposes. Examples include the creation of artwork (one of which was auctioned at Christie's), captions for images, clothing designs, speech, music, and logos.

Despite all this, the GAN is not without its problems. Perhaps the most notable one is deepfakes. This is where images or videos are manipulated for nefarious purposes, such as to make it look like people are saying something they never said.

There are also some technical issues with the GAN. Note that the parameters can be temperamental and this could result in data that looks undifferentiated. A GAN also requires large amounts of computing power.

Reinforcement Learning

Earlier in the chapter, we covered reinforcement learning and how it has been critical for cutting-edge developments in AI, such as with learning to become super game players. Now let's get a deeper understanding of the technology.

The technique is a form of unsupervised learning. And a key principal of reinforcement learning is that it learns by using a reward-punishment system. This is one of the reasons reinforcement learning is so effective with games. Initially there are random moves testing the environment. If an action results in getting points, then the algorithm will emphasize this. But of course, if another move results in a penalty, say running into an obstacle or losing energy, this will be avoided. Reinforcement learning is about trial and error.

With sophisticated models like AlphaGo, this process is done with millions of simulations and usually requires a tremendous amount of computing power (the most advanced models can easily have over 100 GPUs). There is also then the combination with deep learning, which adds to the effectiveness. This is called deep reinforcement learning.

But games are certainly not the only use cases. Reinforcement learning has been a good approach for areas like

- *Robotics*: The machine can learn as it navigates an unknown environment. For example, Google built a robot that learned how to walk within about two hours.[14]

- *Immersive experiences*: Startup rct studio, for example, uses reinforcement learning to generate rich data sets so as to help create life-like virtual environments. "For entertainment, the future consists of freeform environments that the next generation of 'movie-goers' and gamers are looking for," said Yuheng Chen, who is the company's Chief Operating Officer. "AI-powered characters will co-adapt to produce elaborate storylines, and consumers will no longer be confined to fixed dialogues and rigid interaction between non-player characters."[15]

[14]https://techcrunch.com/2020/05/05/the-future-of-deep-reinforcement-learning-our-contemporary-ai-superhero/
[15]From the author's interview with Yuheng Chen on May 22, 2020.

- *Robotic Process Automation (RPA)*: RPA is software that automates tedious and repetitive business processes. In terms of reinforcement learning, it can help create bots that can identify and optimize processes.

- *Investments*: Reinforcement learning can be used to analyze real-time data to keep improving the predictive power of the model, helping to produce better returns.

Some of the advantages for reinforcement learning are the following: the errors are fixed as they occur; there is exploration of the data, which helps to detect more meaningful patterns; and it tends to work well in complex environments. On other hand, the approach usually requires large data sets and the models can get overloaded, resulting in inaccuracies.

Deep Learning

Earlier in the chapter, we took a look at some of the history of deep learning and the applications. In this section, we'll take a more detailed view of the topic.

"Because deep learning excels at identifying patterns in unstructured data, enterprises can use it to unlock the value of data they already have, revealing patterns they can use to create or improve products and services," said Brent Schroeder, who is the Chief Technology Officer at SUSE. "For example, a deep learning model that combines a customer's search queries, browsing history, news preferences, and movie and TV show rankings can provide a more accurate purchase suggestion. Personalized recommendations on a shopping website can improve a retailer's competitive advantage as well as their customer relationship management."[16]

How does this work? At the center of deep learning is a neural network, which takes in data, training it to find patterns, and then produces output. Each of the neurons process the data and they are represented on three parts: input layer, the hidden layer, and the output layer. Figure 2-12 shows this.

---

[16]This is from the author's interview of Brent Schroeder on April 22, 2020.

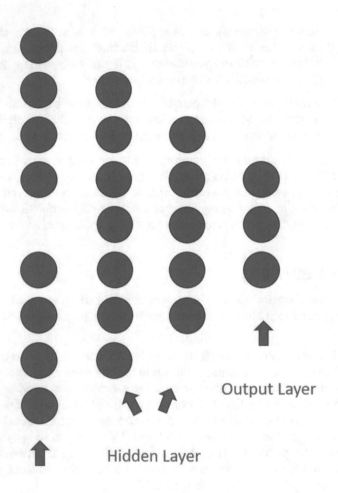

Output Layer

Hidden Layer

Input Layer

Figure 2-12. This shows the input layer, the hidden layer, and the output layer for a neural network

In Figure 2-12, the circles represent the neurons, which make the calculations, although the neurons within the hidden layer do most of the work.

Suppose you want to create a neural network that recognizes a number. So you feed it 3 and the different pixels are embedded in the input neurons for the input layer. There can be quite a few and they will be represented by a notation like X_1 (to make things simple, you will not use all the pixels in this example). Here it is in Figure 2-13.

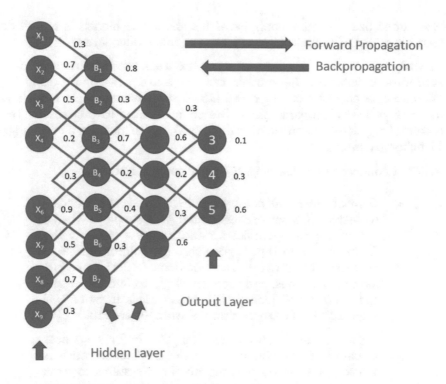

Figure 2-13. This shows a neural network that has processed data

You can see in this illustration that the neurons are connected to each other. And as is the case with the human brain, the connections have different levels of strength, which are represented by a numerical weight that ranges from 0 to 1. When the neural network ingests the data for the number 3, it is sent to the layer that has neurons that are called a bias (this is denoted by B). Then there are calculations with an activation function and this determines if a neuron should be turned on and the data passed through other layers. This process is called forward propagation. After all this, there are weights for the output layer. The one with the highest will be the value selected. In this example, this is 5 because it has a weight of 0.6 (this means there is a 60% chance this is the correct answer).

But the neural network came up with the wrong conclusion! However, the neural network will account for the error and then send this data back to the input layer, which is a process called backpropagation. A neural network will involve an interaction of forward propagation and backpropagation to get more accurate results.

How does deep learning apply here? It's about the hidden layers. A deep learning model will usually have at least a couple hidden layers.

As deep learning is often used for complex areas like facial recognition and autonomous vehicles, the models can get extremely complex and large. Microsoft developed a library called DeepSpeed that can train models with more than 100 billion parameters. The company used it to create its Turing Natural Language Generation model (T-NLG), which included a mind-bogging 17 billion parameters.[17]

When it comes to deep learning, there are some variations:

- *Convolutional neural networks (CNNs)*: This is about finding something in a set of messy data. An example is when a self-driving car identifies a pedestrian. As for how the CNN would do this, it goes through different levels of processing the data called convolutions. At first, it may just look for the lines, and then it will try to find the shape, and then it will identify the object. This iteration will eventually lead to recognition of what we are looking for.

- *Recurrent neural networks (RNNs)*: This is for sequences of data like a document or a series of numbers, such as stock prices. To do this, the RNN has systems to track the data, such as with a memory cell (the most recent data gets the most emphasis), and to allow for feedback loops. This type of deep learning approach has been useful for understanding language, creating captions for images, self-driving cars, supply-chain management, and stock market predictions. But RNNs are usually more susceptible to the vanishing gradient problem, which we'll describe next. Yet techniques like LSTM (long short term memory network) have been able to help.

Even though deep learning has been quite effective and has seen cutting-edge breakthroughs in AI, there are still some issues to consider. Usually you need large amounts of data and heavy computing power.

Another issue is the vanishing gradient problem. This means that, as more layers and parameters are added, the model can show deteriorating results.

And finally, deep learning is often a black box. "Even scientists who develop highly sophisticated neural networks can't clearly define how the neural network arrived at the result," said Brian Cha, who is a Product Manager and

---

[17]https://syncedreview.com/2020/02/12/17-billion-parameters-microsoft-deepspeed-breeds-worlds-largest-nlp-model/

Deep Learning Evangelist at FLIR Systems. "This can be particularly problematic in applications that require such documentation, such as for FDA approval of drugs and medical devices."[18]

Natural Language Processing

Natural language processing (NLP) is perhaps one of the most common ways people interact with AI. It's a core technology that allows for apps like Apple's Siri and Amazon's Alexa to operate. However, NLP is not just about voice communication. It also covers written content.

Regardless, there are two main elements for NLP:

- *Natural language understanding (NLU)*: This decodes the words and then tries to comprehend their meanings. To do this, a computer needs to preprocess the text, which means translating the words and parts of words into numerical values with techniques like tokenization, stemming, and lemmatization.

- *Natural language generation (NLG)*: Once the NLP system understands the input, it will then need to find ways to respond in plain English (or whatever the language required).

Until the 1990s, NLP systems were crude and not very useful. The main reason was that that they were based on rules-based approaches (similar to what we covered with expert systems, earlier in the chapter). But the researchers realized that machine learning could make NLP much better and more powerful. The result has been an ongoing improvement in the quality. With the emergence of deep learning and the work of companies like Google, the technology has accelerated.

Despite this, there is still a long way to go. For example, when just looking at the English language, there are many nuances and vague meanings. In a typical conversation, there may be a myriad of assumptions, fast talk, different tones, and body language. It is also common to not be grammatically correct and to use slang. Oh, and then there are the accents and dialects!

The English language is also dynamic, as new words are added frequently. Then there are the complexities with domain-specific words, especially in categories like healthcare.

---

[18]From the author's interview with Brian Cha on April 12, 2020.

To see a real-world case study of NLP, let's consider a company called Capacity. The company has leveraged AI to redefine the traditional helpdesk, such as with the automation of support for customers and employees. Capacity's system essentially learns as it processes the interactions. The goal is to resolve issues before a ticket is even created, which means that employees have more time to devote to important tasks and that there are higher levels of customer satisfaction.

One of the companies that has implemented Capacity is West Community Credit Union (WCCU), which is a Missouri-based bank with nine branches, $260 million in assets, and 25,000 members. The company wanted to use AI to greatly increase the experience and to add more value to every part of the process, from handling a loan to better management of client money.

With Capacity, WCCU uploaded a knowledge base and the AI took things over. The result was that more than 90% of the questions received were answered without a team member getting involved. And by adding more information to the NLP bot, there was an increase in converting prospects to customers.

"A lot of smaller organizations assume two things about AI," said David Karandish, who is the CEO of Capacity. "First, they assume that it's complex and challenging to use, and requires months to implement. With Capacity's solution, you're up and running in a few days and it's as easy to use as email or Slack. Second, most smaller organizations assume they won't see the ROI of implementing AI technology. While the idea of automation can be intimidating, a user-friendly AI that can quickly help your team do its best work is worth the investment."

Conclusion

This has definitely been a long chapter. This is not to imply you need to know everything covered. Hey, even experts in the AI field usually have knowledge of certain areas.

The key is to understand that AI is a major category with a myriad of subsets. And machine learning is one of the most important when it comes to business applications. The other thing to remember is that there often needs to be lots of data for the models to be effective.

In the next chapter, we will take a look at the first step in the AI process: identifying the problem to be solved.

Key Takeaways

- AI is far from a new field. The roots go back to the 1930s.

- It was during a conference in 1956 that AI become more formalized. It's also when the world's first application, called the Logic Theorist, was introduced.

- In the early years of AI, much of the financial support came from the federal government, primarily because of the focus on the Cold War and the Apollo space program.

- The years from 1956 to 1974 were known as the Golden Age of AI. But unfortunately, after this came the AI Winter. It was a time when the federal government began to cut back on funding. This would not be the only AI Winter either.

- Despite the waning interest, there continued to be innovation with AI. One example of this was the emergence of expert systems, which were based on codifying knowledge of certain industries like healthcare.

- The Turing Test is a thought experiment created by the legendary mathematician Alan Turing. It's a way to see if a machine can think. He did not base it on any benchmarks. Rather, it was about whether a person believed that they were really interacting with another person, not a machine.

- In the early 1980s, John Searle wrote an influential paper that tried to debunk the Turing Test. He also said there were two types of AI: strong AI, which was where machines could truly think, and weak AI, which was where technology is applied to a narrow purpose.

- AI is an wide-ranging topic. It has different subsets like machine learning, deep learning, and natural language processing.

- Machine learning processes data to help make better decisions. There are different ways to do this, including supervised learning, unsupervised learning, semi-supervised learning, and reinforcement learning.

- Supervised learning is the most common approach of machine learning and involves the use of labeled data. There are two main approaches: regression (this uses output variables that are continuous like weight or money) and classification (this divides the data into different groupings). Some of the algorithms that can do this include linear/multiple regression, logistic regression, support vector machines, random forests, K-nearest neighbor, and Naïve Bayes classifiers.

- Unsupervised learning is used when there is no labeled data. Instead, sophisticated algorithms try to infer patterns. Some of the approaches include clustering, anomaly detection, association, and autoencoders.

- Semi-supervised learning is where there is a mix of labeled and unlabeled data. By using algorithms, it's possible to create labeled data to fill the gaps.

- Reinforcement learning is based on a reward-punishment system. Essentially, the algorithm learns by trial and error.

- Deep learning is based on a neural network, which processes data through an input layer, hidden layers, and an output layer. By iterating through this, there is usually improved accuracy.

- NLP is used to process language, whether written or spoken. Moreover, deep learning has certainly been important for the rapid improvement in accuracy. But there is still a long way to go.

Identify the Problem to Be Solved

Where do you start with your AI project?

Ken Xie, who was born in China, is one of the most successful entrepreneurs in Silicon Valley. His focus has been on transforming cybersecurity technology, such as by developing the first ASIC-based firewall and VPM appliance in the 1990s.

He also started several breakout companies. There was NetScreen, which was sold to Cisco for $4 billion in 2004. Then he co-founded Fortinet, which has seen consistently strong growth (the other co-founder was his brother, Michael). The market value is about $22.5 billion and there are more than 450,000 customers across the globe.

Then what about AI? What has the company done with this technology? It has definitely been a major priority. In fact, AI has been essential in not only improving cybersecurity systems but also in dealing with the talent shortage of skilled technical employees.

© Tom Taulli 2021
T. Taulli, *Implementing AI Systems*, https://doi.org/10.1007/978-1-4842-6385-3_3

"The cybersecurity skills gap is very real and hasn't shown signs of improving in the foreseeable future," said Derek Manky, who is the Chief of Security Insights and Global Threat Alliances at FortiGuard Labs, which is a division of Fortinet. "At the same time, the threat landscape is becoming more complex, posing significant risk for just about any organization. For example, and specific to AI, in recent years, the security industry has seen cybercriminals investing in weaponizing AI for their own nefarious activities, developing AI-based attacks. For those organizations that have the right technology in place, AI has emerged as the ultimate tool for cybersecurity professionals to close the skills gap and 'fight fire with fire' against prolific hackers already using AI technology."

To this end, Fortinet has invested heavily in creating self-learning deep neural networks to essentially act like a virtual security analyst that investigates attacks. At the heart of this is a patent-pending algorithm that is based on more than 20 million clean and malicious files, and has classified the threats into more than 20 attack scenarios.

"When leveraging Fortinet's AI technology, what would have traditionally taken a cybersecurity expert a few days to narrow down, AI can detect in minutes or sub-seconds," said Manky.

For Fortinet, AI is an ongoing process and requires a strong commitment of resources. "Learning is a long game, and is always evolving and the main task—both for internal processes, pipelines, and customer protection—is always reducing the workload and working smarter," said Manky. "Machine learning is specific to a task. The largest model we have is filtering malicious codeblocks from code, which we started supervised training about over five years ago. We have billions of features mined from our 800 million malware samples, as a result, making the model more precise and acceptable to deploy to production."

True, Fortinet has some inherent advantages when it comes to AI. The company has many talented data scientists and researchers. There is also the benefit of large data sets (the company gets more than two million virus samples a day).

But even with all this, success has definitely not been a sure thing. The company understands that AI is not about science experiments; rather, it should solve real-world business problems.

And yes this is what we will focus on in this chapter. So let's get started.

Buy vs. Build?

It's tempting to want to get started quickly on an AI project. The technology is exciting and innovative. There is also the opportunity to transform the organization.

So who wouldn't be motivated?

No doubt, the enthusiasm is understandable. But it is also critical that there be patience, planning, and deliberation. AI is not easy and as you've already seen in this book, risk of failure is considerable.

This is why you need to have a compelling case for the technology—that is, how it can solve a problem. This is something that needs to be clear and deep.

And even if you identify a problem to be solved, this does not mean you should necessarily have a project either.

The question should instead be, is there an off-the-shelf AI offering that will work? If so, then this is the way to go. It will certainly minimize the risks.

The good news is that there are a myriad of third-party AI applications and they keep coming onto the market. Many are also easy to implement and use. Even the pricing is usually affordable. Actually, in some cases, the technology is free, such as with open source solutions.

Something else to note: Your existing applications may already have strong AI capabilities. So make sure you know what they are and get the most out of them. This is perhaps the most impactful way to get started with AI.

Here are a few examples of widely used software applications that have powerful AI features:

- *Workday*: The company is a pioneer in cloud-based ERP (enterprise resource planning) and its applications help with areas like human resources and accounting. To bolster its AI capabilities, Workday has been aggressive in its acquisitions. In 2016, the company acquired Platfora (a big data operator) and then a couple years later, it spent $1.55 billion for Adaptive Insights (the company is focused on analytics for finance).[1] As a result, Workday has been rolling out a variety of AI systems. For example, there is one called the Skills Cloud, which helps with hiring, training, and team building. Then there is a natural language generation (NLG) app that automatically creates descriptions based on analysis of transactions on the Workday platform. According to the company's CEO and co-founder, Aneel Bhusri: "If the last 15 years of the cloud have been about moving business processes from on-premise to the cloud and making it easier, friendlier, and better, I think the next 15 years is about using your

[1] www.zdnet.com/article/workday-unifies-approach-to-machine-learning-analytics-and-planning/

data to make better business decisions. Machine learning is really the cornerstone set of technologies that help you understand your data, find insight in your data, and help you make better business decisions that will hopefully lead to better business results."[2]

- *Microsoft*: Over the years, the company has been retooling its software applications for AI. Just take a look at Office 365, which continues to see more and more functions added. There is Play My Emails for Outlook that highlights the important points for messages as well as Scheduler, which understands your upcoming meetings based on interactions and emails.[3] A cool command is to type "Find a time for us" and the AI will figure things out. Next, PowerPoint has the Presenter Coach. With it, you can do a dry-run of your presentation and the AI will process your voice in real-time, providing helpful suggestions.

- *Einstein*: This is the AI system that is integrated on the Salesforce.com platform. It's quite easy to create a model, such as for predicting sales, churn, lead conversions, and so on. After all, you have seamless access to the data and there are prebuilt models. Einstein also makes the deployment and monitoring process fairly straightforward.

When first evaluating AI for an organization, here's an approach to take, which should help mitigate some the risks:

- *Assess*: Do a good assessment of your current IT assets. What are the AI capabilities? How can they help your company? Does it seem like the software vendor has AI as a priority and that there should be more innovation in the future?

- *Third parties*: If the assessment shows gaps, the next step is to search the market for AI providers. Granted, there are many companies to choose from. But even just a simple Google search can be a good way to filter some of the top ones. An example is "Top AI chatbot startups." There are various sites that provide reviews of software, like G2.com or Trust Radius.

---

[2]www.cxotalk.com/episode/workday-ceo-machine-learning-enterprise-software
[3]https://venturebeat.com/2019/12/31/6-ai-features-microsoft-added-to-office-in-2019/

- *Project*: If the first two steps do not provide what you are looking for, then this is the point to give serious consideration to putting together your own AI project. And in much of this book, I'll show how to do this.

Now keep in mind that a third-party AI solution will likely have its downsides. Let's face it, even the top software companies do not have the resources to address all use cases. No technology is a cure-all.

Yet often third-party software will be good enough. For the most part, putting together an in-house AI project is expensive, time consuming, and risky. So before making this commitment, you definitely want to put lots of effort into looking at the alternatives.

When evaluating a third-party solution, here are some of the factors to consider:

- *Backing*: You want a company with sufficient resources to invest in R&D. This is why it is important for there to be financial backing, such as from venture capitalists.

- *Vertical*: Does the software company have experience in your industry? The results of AI can vary widely based on the vertical.

- *Security*: Look to see what the software has done in terms of protecting data and complying with regulations.

- *Customization*: How much flexibility is there in the software? Can you create your own models? Are AI tools integrated into the platform?

- *ROI*: Try to get a rough estimate on the return. If the AI software works, what are the benefits, such as in cost savings or improving the customer experience? Are these enough to justify the costs of the license of the technology and any consulting for the implementation?

Of course, some of these factors may be more important than others. Because of this, you might come up with a score sheet, in which you assign points for the criteria. This can help you make comparisons across different AI solutions.

Interestingly enough, even if there are strong third-party solutions, there may be cases when you still might want to do a project. This could be if it is highly strategic and you want to build your own proprietary IP (intellectual property). As a result, this could wind up being a valuable asset for a potential funding, acquisition, or IPO.

Here are some other reasons:

- You want something that is flexible enough to allow for ongoing evolution of the model.

- You might have strict data requirements and may not want the corporate information to be on a third-party cloud.

In this buy-versus-build process, there is another question you need to ask: Is AI the right approach? Given the hype surrounding this technology, it is understandable that there is an inclination to use AI for just about everything. But the fact is that the technology is only useful for certain use cases. Often, when it comes to solving problems, a simpler approach can be taken. Or there may be a traditional app that gets the job done.

Where to Start?

OK, after you have determined that building your own AI solution is the right approach, then comes another very difficult decision: identifying what problem to solve. At this stage, it's a good idea to be free-flowing and open minded about the idea. This could mean setting up a workshop for the day and assembling a diverse group of technical and non-technical people from across the organization. To make this more productive, there should also be a primer on AI. This could be a small document or perhaps a video that describes the technology, what it can do, and how other companies have used it.

Regardless, when it comes to the workshop, there should be little criticism or pushback on suggestions. You want an environment where people feel they can be creative. At the end of the workshop, you can list the ideas.

Then comes the filtering stage. Here is a suggested approach:

- *Data*: This is perhaps the most important factor for AI. Data is what powers sophisticated algorithms—and there is often a need for large amounts of data. Thus, before deciding on where to focus your AI efforts, make sure you have access to the right data. What's more, even if you have a good source, there could still be trouble. Of course, it's common for there to be turf wars when it comes to access to data. Or there could be issues with privacy, especially with personally identifiable data.

- *Start small*: For your first AI project, it's usually best to have a focused area to build the model. For example, suppose someone suggests using the technology to improve the company's invoice processing. While this would certainly be helpful, it would probably be too much of an effort. Instead, you might want to do something like look at how AI can help process invoices for a particular type of customer. In other words, by doing this, you will not only get results quicker, but also not have to deal with lots of complexity, which can easily bog down a project. Strive for quick wins.

- *Low-hanging fruit*: Yes, this is definitely a good place to start. In terms of AI, this means looking at tasks or processes that are repetitive or tedious. Usually they are the easiest to automate and to get quick returns on investment. On the other hand, avoid areas that involve deep thinking and judgment. AI is generally not good at these tasks.

- *Risk takers*: Look for those departments or teams that are known for being risk takers and are amenable to new technologies. This is will definitely get the AI project off to the right start.

- *Integrations*: An AI project usually needs to be integrated with a variety of other technologies, say CRMs, ERPs, and so on. This is why it is important to see what is needed to make the algorithms work with these systems. In some cases, there may be considerable work with the current legacy IT environment.

After you have found the area to focus on, then you can set up a workflow. This could be in the form of a visual, such as a flowchart. And each decision point should be documented. This will be a great help to the data scientists because they will have a clear-cut roadmap for the development.

It's also recommended to put together a time table. True, it will likely change. But this is fine. The goal is to provide more structure on the AI development process but also help to incentivize faster action.

Finally, you should put together a KPI (key performance indicator), which is the measure of the success of the project. Again, it will probably be subject to change. But a KPI will be another key in moving the project forward and creating momentum.

A common KPI for AI is for hours saved. This is certainly easy to calculate and is important for any organization. But there are some other KPIs to consider, like

- *NPS (Net Promotor Score)*: This is a popular way to measure customer satisfaction and is based on one question: "How likely is it that you would recommend us to a friend or colleague?" So with AI, the KPI would be to achieve some level of increase in NPS. Even a small one could have a major impact.

- *Revenue*: This is perhaps the KPI that creates the most interest in an AI program. Who doesn't want to get more revenue, right? Definitely. The good news is that AI can be particularly useful for this purpose. This is especially the case with areas like finding opportunities for cross-selling, targeting better prospects, and improving pricing (which we'll look at later in this chapter).

- *Risk management*: AI can monitor for anomalies on a 24/7 basis and also get smarter about identifying them. This can be a big help for fraud detection or even to provide for safety in harsh physical environments.

Something else that is critical for an AI project is to have a clear question. A blog post from Marco Casalaina, who is the VP of Products at Salesforce Einstein, shows how to approach this.[4]

Let's take a look:

- *Yes-or-no question*: Will there be churn? Is this lead a good one? You then set up the criteria to answer the question. This could be that, if there is at least a 40% chance of churn, then the answer would be "yes."

- *Numerical question*: How much will revenue increase if Jane becomes a customer? How much will sales fall if the price of the product is increased by 20%?

- *Matching*: This is about recommending something, such as a product to a user or an email to a prospect.

By having a question, you will be in a much better position to focus the project on what is important and this should lead to much better results. As noted in the Salesforce blog: "You have to know where you're going before you decide on the best way to get there. Successful AI solutions also come at the problem

---

[4]www.salesforce.com/blog/2019/06/how-to-get-started-with-ai.html

with a unique point of view. You have to be able to answer the questions around why traditional software can't solve the problem, and why AI can."

AI Consultants

DataRobot is the developer of an AI platform that helps streamlines the process. The company has raised over $430 million.

Note that a major part of the growth strategy has been to acquire different companies to bolster the capabilities. While many are technology startups, there was one that did not fit this mold. In June 2020, DataRobot purchased SOURCE AI from the Boston Consulting Group (BCG). The division was founded to provide advisory services and resources to help data scientists write AI systems.

What was interesting about this deal was that it highlighted the importance of professional services. The fact is that—despite all the strides in automation technologies—AI remains quite challenging, especially when putting together a project. The data and modelling work can be quite challenging, time consuming, and expensive.

According to the press release for the DataRobot-BCG transaction: "[The] relationship between a global consulting firm and an AI solution provider is an industry first that combines proprietary IP with leading consulting services, thus providing both the human expertise and the technical know-how needed to deliver optimal, continuous value from AI."[5]

So then it should be no surprise that many organizations use a consultant or consulting firms when putting together an AI project.

Here are just some of the benefits:

- *Speed*: You don't want your competitors to get an edge. But if you have several failed projects, this can easily happen. This is why retaining a consulting firm can be so essential. You get the benefit of experience and knowledge to avoid the problems. For the most part, there is a focus on what is impactful.

- *Diversity*: There are a myriad of algorithms and approaches to AI. But when you hire a data scientist, you will likely get someone who has expertise in a narrow area. Yet this may be less of a problem with a consulting firm since you have access to an assortment of AI experts with varied backgrounds.

---

[5]www.businesswire.com/news/home/20200609005183/en/DataRobot-Acquires-Boston-Consulting-Group%E2%80%99s-SOURCE-AI

- *Recruiting*: This is always difficult, regardless of the position. But when it comes to a complex area like AI, the recruiting process can be much more difficult. With a consulting firm, you do not have to go through this process.

- *Commitment*: A consulting arrangement does not have to be a long-term one. It can actually be a way to get quick learnings about AI. Once the organization is more comfortable with the technology, there can be an effort to form an in-house team.

- *Assessment*: A consulting firm can evaluate your current organization and IT resources. From this, it can then provide a more objective assessment on what needs to be done. A consulting firm can often uncover problems or advantages that may not necessarily be obvious.

- *Vendor evaluation*: Buying software for AI is tricky. There is also the consideration of when it makes sense to use open source software. A consulting firm should have experience with the existing solutions on the market and can help better navigate the selection process.

- *Proprietary AI technology*: Some consulting firms have built their own systems. This can be incredibly valuable for a client.

- *Training*: To get real value from AI, there is a need for extensive education. A consulting firm may have curriculum and instructors for this.

- *Long-term*: A good consulting firm will help to build a solid foundation that will allow for the AI system to evolve over time. A firm can also be helpful in putting in place ways for change management so there will be ongoing adoption and scaling of the technology.

On the other hand, hiring a consulting firm is not without its considerable risks. It can be extremely difficult to know the track record and performance.

The costs can also be hefty. There is really not an alignment of interests. Hey, a consulting firm will want to expand its relationship and be a partner for many years, right? This is true. But this may not necessarily be the goal of the client.

This is why it's important to spend time vetting a consulting firm. Do a Google search and ask people in your network, such as on LinkedIn. You also want to get references.

However, there is something else you should do: make sure your organization is prepared for a consulting firm. First of all, you should identify any data you have available and put together a list of those people in the organization that have data science backgrounds. You should also identify those people who have domain expertise for the problem you want to solve. Next, you can put together a requirements document, which will set forth the objectives for your AI project and the time table.

And what about the fees? It's typical that there will be a fixed per-project price or an hourly/daily amount. In some cases, a consulting firm may even use value-based fees. That is, it will get a percentage of the savings derived from the project.

Regardless of the approach, it is important to have contractual clauses that allow you to end the arrangement if the requirements are not met. If the consultant is hesitant with this, this is a major red flag.

Let's take a look at some examples of how consulting firms have helped clients with their AI projects:

- *Banking*: A national commercial bank acquired a rival. But there was a problem: the company had a large amount of unstructured PDFs for the loan documents. Deloitte was retained to assess the situation, and the firm implemented its own propriety D-ICE Natural Language Solution, which uses sophisticated OCR (optical character recognition). The result was $20 million in new revenue opportunities.[6]

- *Healthcare*: A client, a large integrated healthcare services company, came to Cognizant to help with lessening drug addiction for certain medical treatments. Keep in mind that US healthcare organizations spend over $500 billion a year on caring for those addicted to opioids. It's incredibly difficult to identify those patients that are susceptible to this risk. The consulting team at Cognizant approached this by using an AI system based on text analytics on physicians' notes with electronic medical records (EMR). As a result, the system was able to provide alerts to doctors during patient visits if there was a certain risk of addiction. In all, it was able to identify over 85,000 patients and save $60 million.[7]

---

[6]www2.deloitte.com/us/en/pages/deloitte-analytics/articles/business-ana-lytics-case-studies.html
[7]www.cognizant.com/case-studies/ai-based-preventive-care

- *Financial services:* A multinational financial services organization based in California wanted to better use its community forum, which was for its developers and vendors to ask questions and resolve issues. The firm hired Infosys for this project. The company also had its own proprietary text analytics platform called HINT that was built on open source software. The community forum was not necessarily large—it had over 35,000 conversations—but it involved complex discussions. As for Infosys, it helped with ingesting the content and training (this was particularly challenging because it was used by multiple users). There was also data labeling. But Infosys was able to put together a PoC (proof-of-concept) in a week and completed the project within a month.[8]

Case Study: Intuit

Founded in 1983, Intuit has been able to manage through major transitions in technology: from DOS to Windows to the Net and to mobile. As for what it sees as its next transition, of course, it is AI. The company actually considers this to be its biggest opportunity in its storied history.

Intuit has the benefit of massive data sets from franchises like Mint, QuickBooks, and TurboTax. The result is that the products have gotten more personalized for each customer.

Take TurboTax. With over 50 million filers, there are major challenges in understanding the needs of its customers. They have unique situations, which can quickly get complicated because of the immense size of the US Tax Code.

"We use AI to route calls and emails to the right person or resource to answer questions," said Ashok Srivastava, who is the Senior Vice President and Chief Data Officer at Intuit. "This process is based on historical information about each customer. We also use AI techniques like NLP, which can help understand intent while the user is typing a question. In fact, the algorithms can understand customer needs even before they ask. This certainly creates a delightful experience."

Srivastava does acknowledge that there are certain areas where AI has fallen short. "NLP is extremely difficult," he said. "People usually do not talk in a precise way. We may imply things that a machine cannot understand. Even scanning documents like W-2s is far from easy. What if there are wrinkles? Bad writing? Information in the wrong box? The irony is that people can spot these very easily. But this is not the case with computers."

---

[8]`www.infosys.com/industries/financial-services/case-studies/leveraging-actionable-insights.html`

However, this does not imply that Srivastava thinks such problems are not solvable. He is definitely optimistic about AI's capabilities. "We are more than a decade in the AI journey," he said. "We are most excited with this technology. It has already shown significant returns."

Case Study: Zilliant

Zilliant, which was founded in 1998, is focused on developing software to help companies better manage their B2B pricing. The company has over 100 global enterprises as customers, which range from manufacturers to distributors to service companies.

While pricing is a critical corporate function, it often does not get much attention. But this can be a big mistake. According to Zilliant's own analysis of B2B transactions, there is margin loss of 1.8% to 13.0% when pricing is overlooked or is underutilized.

So why does pricing get short shrift? There are a variety of reasons:

- *Ownership*: The pricing function is often spread across the organization, not a centralized team. Because of this, it can be tough to have a good strategy and maintain consistency.

- *Complexity*: There are a myriad of components for pricing, including competitive conditions, customer size, order size, regional factors, costs, and so on. This is why it is common that companies rely on rules-of-thumb or simple calculations. But this can easily mean problems, especially when salespeople engage in discounting on an ad hoc basis.

- *Data*: Companies may think that they do not have enough quality data for sophisticated algorithms to optimize pricing.

As for Zilliant's own solution, it is based on a cloud-native multi-tenant SaaS architecture, which has an assortment of modules (Price IQ, Price Manager, Sales IQ, Sales Planner, Deal Manager, Cart IQ, and IQ Anywhere). There is also a sophisticated infrastructure of microservices that help with customization and integration. And there is quite a bit of AI built into the platform, which can even be accessible with a Jupyter notebook.

"There is a wide swath of AI and machine learning in use within the IQ Platform, including random forest, neural net, association rules, k-means, and natural language processing," said Pete Eppele, who is the Senior Vice President of Products and Science at Zilliant.[9] "Price IQ has the unique ability among price optimization vendors to measure price elasticity in B2B and has a constraint-based approach to optimization, called convex optimization. This 'crystal box' pricing science is easy to understand and interact with to tailor pricing strategies and use price as a strategic business lever. Sales IQ utilizes clustering algorithms and predictive sales analytics to create purchase pattern profiles that identify 'ideal' customers and then match customers to the best fit profile to pinpoint cross-sell opportunities and spot the early signs of defection."

However, when it comes to implementing the AI, the process does take some time. There often needs to be integration, data wrangling, and learning for the algorithms. So expect anywhere from 4 to 12 weeks for Zilliant to get effectively deployed. To help this along, the company has a professional services team.

The following are examples of how the system is used:

- *Building products manufacturer*: The company implemented an AI-driven pricing model tailored to its complex product line. The result: There was a 1.3% increase in margin.

- *Large distributor of lubricants and chemicals*: The company's market was getting more competitive and there was a need to find ways to boost profitability. It used Zilliant for its 2,000 products to create a predictive sales model, which changed the pricing to improve cross-sell opportunities as well as to detect early signs of churn. By doing this, there was a 94% adoption rate for the opportunities and incremental revenue gains of $5 million.

Yet this is not to imply that the success was due mostly to technology. "For pricing AI to succeed and show value, there needs to be collaboration with the in-house experts in pricing and sales," said Eppele. "It's this 'experts plus equations' formula that's critical to deliver real, sustained value. Math alone won't get you there. Pricing is a human and emotional process. If you're going to use AI to set pricing, ensure the pricing is explainable and believable by skeptics. It also needs to consider inputs outside the data to drive maximum value."

---

[9]From the author's interview with Pete Eppele on June 6, 2020.

Case Study: Halliburton

Halliburton Energy Services is one of the world's largest oil services companies and has about 50,000 employees across more 80 countries. The company helps with large and complex projects, and they often require sophisticated technologies.

To facilitate this, the company relies on a myriad of third-party software platforms, such as MathWorks. This company has actually been around since the mid-1980s and is a pioneer in developing tools for analytics and machine learning. MathWorks also has an extensive consulting service arm to help clients with the implementations and maintenance.

A key to the software is that it has a strong collaboration function, helping to connect employees, customers, and the supply chain. This is certainly essential when running AI and machine learning models.

"Too many organizations focus mostly on developing those algorithms," said Paul Pilotte, who is the AI Technical Marketing Lead at MathWorks. "But, ultimately, they are delivering a product or a service to the market that is based on AI. They are not delivering an AI algorithm. To successfully deliver that AI-driven product, they need to incorporate AI across the entire system design workflow."

Regarding Halliburton, the company looked to MathWorks to help build an AI system to improve safety with oil drilling operations. For example, there is a need to use explosives from a perforating gun to allow oil into the well bore. Thus, it is important to know if they have been detonated before they are brought back up to the surface and removed from the well.

This is not an easy thing to do because there needs to be interpretation of sound data. And the sounds can be two or three miles underground. True, Halliburton used accelerometers to better capture the signals. But there was the problem of other noise, such as from generators and pumps.

This is where AI could help out—that is, to filter out the background data. With MathWorks, Halliburton created a neural network model, which included the Deep Learning Toolbox, to get the right results. This was also turned into an application that could be deployed on a laptop and used at a well site.

"While AI commonly uses image data to create models, Halliburton highlights using signal data with a deep learning/AI model," said Pilotte. "Being able to remove noise from signals would traditionally require expertise in signal processing. This AI model can automatically learn to identify the noise and remove it automatically. This highlights one of many new applications that AI can be used to improve on traditional methods."

Case Study: Cadence

Cadence came about from a merger in 1988 between Solomon Design Automation and ECAD, which were pioneers of electronic design automation (EDA). This involves the development of sophisticated software tools to help create electronic systems like semiconductors and circuit boards. Currently Cadence generates $2.34 billion in revenues and has about 8,100 employees across 21 countries.

In 2018, the company's management looked to see how AI could transform their organization. This was initially sparked with a hackathon, in which anyone could contribute ideas for interesting applications. All in all, it was a great success. But Cadence followed this up with training and ongoing support for projects.

In terms of the AI applications, the company has been able to implement the technology in its own toolsets so as to improve the testing, diagnostics, and development of chipsets. The system even provides suggestions to improve designs. Interestingly enough, the user often does not know that AI is being used for this!

As chip technologies get more advanced and intricate, such as with smaller 7 nanometer chips, the development process can be time consuming. But with AI, Cadence has been able to reduce the time-to-market, which is a huge benefit to customers.

Note that the improvement can be quite significant. With AI, there has been 77% better TNS (total negative slack), 3.4% less leakage power, and 5% improved WNS (worst negative slack). All of these are key metrics in the chip world.

But Cadence has used AI for areas beyond its design tools. An example is a support portal that automates the answering of questions based on the company's knowledge base.

Case Study: Behavioral Signals

In 2016, Alex Potamianos and Shri Narayanan founded Behavioral Signals because they thought that AI could be used to process emotion. They would go on to build and obtain patents on processes like speech-to-emotion systems. This was all part of a sophisticated API called Oliver, which included a myriad of use cases like virtual assistants, smart speakers, social robots, and interactive toys.

A case study of this is a national EU (European Union) bank that wanted to bolster its fintech capabilities. With Oliver, the company was able to better interpret customer sentiment and attitudes, such as by analyzing pitch and tonal variance of the audio instead of the actual words spoken.

Here are some of the results:

- 20% increase in active debt restructuring applications
- $7.5M of additional restructured debt
- $300M annual upside for the bank
- $1.5M upside per agent per year
- Lower costs because of 7.6% fewer calls

"Behavioral Signals' Behavioral Profile Pairing (BPP) solution, as it was also applied at the EU bank, involves building profiles of customers and call-center agents based on past interactions," said Rana Gujral, who is the CEO of Behavioral Signals. "These profiles are fed into a predictive model to determine which agent should be paired with a specific customer in the future so that the desired outcome is achieved. Behavioral profiles comprise a set of behavior- and emotion-related metrics reflecting, for example, whether a customer is negative, polite, or they have shown any tendency to get easily agitated. Measurements of this kind are extracted from patterns identified in one's voice and are based on emotion AI, namely the capability of the machine to understand the emotional state and intentions of humans. The predictive model that is employed assesses the compatibility of all possible profile pairs and makes specific recommendations regarding who should speak to whom in a given context. It is an example of limited memory AI and has been trained using machine learning and a few thousand past interactions associated with the corresponding outcomes. Fine-tuning the model is also possible and can lead to maximizing a specific KPI of interest, as, for example, customer's propensity to buy in an inside sales call."[10]

Case Study: Phrasee

Can AI write better than people? Maybe not now. So James Patterson and Stephen King should not worry much!

But there is still considerable progress with AI-based writing, which is often based on principles of natural language generation. And much of the innovation has been with business writing. For example, there is a startup called Phrasee (the company was founded in 2015). Just some of the customers include eBay, Domino's, and JOANN.

The Phrasee system essentially creates marketing copy, such as coming up with email subject lines, push notifications, and even Facebook ads—all in real time.

---

[10]From the author's interview with Rana Gujral on June 8, 2020.

"There are two main AI components to Phrasee's technology," said Parry Malm, who is the CEO and co-founder of Phrasee. "NLG, which actually produces language, writes human-sounding marketing copy at the touch of a button—and in a brand's voice; and then there is a deep learning engine that predicts what language will and won't work with greater accuracy than any human. This removes human bias from the equation. Combining these two technologies provides the solution. You brief the system through a simple form, and the system generates thousands upon thousands of copy variants. Then, the deep learning engine selects language that it determines to be the best."[11]

Even a small increase in conversion rates can have a big impact on the bottom line. To see how, take a look at Domino's Pizza. The company used Phrasee for its email promotions, and the average open rate uplift was 26% and the average click rate jumped by 57%.

Case Study: Lex Machina

The roots of Lex Machina are from Stanford's Law School and Computer Science department. The company also got the backing of LexisNexis, a top information provider to the legal industry.

This has certainly been a powerful combination. Lex Machina has become a pioneer of legal analytics so as to help improve strategies, win more legal cases, and close more business. The technology is based on cutting-edge aspects of machine learning and NLP that process huge amounts of information about lawsuits and other litigation data. With all this, it is possible to make much better predictions for legal outcomes.

"With legal data, we always need a path to correct machine mistakes," said Karl Harris, who is the CEO of Lex Machina. "This requirement has significant implications for the overall system, as some NLP/AI techniques don't allow for discrete corrections. Furthermore, we want each correction to have leverage. In other words, we want the system to learn from the corrections that we make. And because the law follows the Federal Rules of Civil Procedure, we're able to embed legal knowledge into our NLP systems to make better choices when evaluating legal data."[12]

One of the customers for Lex Machina is James Yoon, who is a senior Partner at WSGR. He is a patent attorney and has litigated over 150 cases and advised more than 50 companies about IP matters. With Lex Machina, he can better understand and model the litigation issues for a pending case. The technology has also made it easier to take quick action, which is critical when it comes to

---

[11]From the author's interview with Parry Malm on June 11, 2020.
[12]From the author's interview with Karl Harris on June 12, 2020.

patent matters. It's not uncommon that—right before an IPO—there will be an IP lawsuit!

With Lex Machina, Yoon can get analysis in minutes about timing, potential damages, and resolution strategies. This information not only helps to prepare for the case but also to put together an accurate budget for the client.

What about help in the courtroom? Lex Machina does this too. There is Motion Metrics, which shows what specific motions to use in front of a District Judge.

Now, all this is not to imply that the focus of the technology is on law firms. Lex Machina has a diverse set of customers that include large corporations like GM, Microsoft, and Eli Lilly.

"When we talk about AI, we're often thinking about automation," said Harris. "In many cases, we want fully automated solutions, such as identifying which attorneys and law firms were involved in cases, because otherwise we wouldn't be able to scale fast enough with our expansion efforts. In other cases, however, we need to invoke what we call technology-assisted human review. AI and automation are great at pattern matching but poor at judgment. Our goal is to take pattern matching out of the hands of humans and solve it with AI, but to leave judgment in the hands of legally trained human experts. This example as applied to Lex Machina is a good generalization to the state of AI generally."

Case Study: Vecna Robotics

Vecna Robotics is a leader in autonomous mobile robots or AMRs. These systems help companies better manage their distribution, warehousing, and manufacturing. Customers include Medline, GEODIS, FedEx Ground, DHL Supply Chain, and MiltonCAT. The company has also raised $63.5 million from venture capitalists, including Blackhorn Ventures, Drive Capital, Tectonic Ventures, Highland Capital Partners, and Fontinalis Partners.

A key to Vecna Robotics is a sophisticated AI system called Pivotal, which integrates with warehouse management and multi-vendor automation platforms. The result is higher throughput, improved operational efficiency, and better human-robot collaboration.

Traditionally, materials handling has relied primarily on people to move goods throughout a warehouse or distribution center. But over the years, companies have been adopting semi-autonomous solutions. While this led to improvements, there were still challenges, especially with the inflexibility of logistic infrastructures.

So what to do? Companies are now starting to deploy AMRs, which can intelligently automate manual tasks without the fixed infrastructure of semi-automated solutions. Examples of the applications include cross-docking, line-side replenishment, transport of oversized SKUs, and staging lane put-away.

"From a customer perspective, Vecna Robotics works with FedEx Ground, one of the world's largest shipping and logistics companies," said Daniel Theobald, who is the CEO of Vecna Robotics. "Across these customer sites, transportation of non-conveyables—oversized shipments such as furniture and car parts—was a very manual process. Some companies have seen the proportion of non-conveyable goods increase from about 8-11% in the last few years, and continues to grow faster today."

To make this happen, Vecna Robotics has invested heavily in AI. For example, the company has developed deep learning models to detect pallets, help with navigation, and deal with avoidance of obstacles. There is also extensive use of simulations, which help to map out the potential scenarios.

"Using AI, we discovered that using a robot to automate manual activities increases productivity by 38%," said Theobald. "Using AI-powered orchestration algorithms as applied to just robots, there was a 57% increase in productivity. With orchestration applied to robots and facility associates, we saw a 116% increase in throughput. This speaks to the future of human-robot collaboration."

Beware of AI Moonshots

From the start when IBM was created back in 1911, the company had a core focus of making bold bets. It always wanted to be at the cutting-edge.

The result has been a wide array of amazing innovations. Consider that the company created the floppy disk, random access memory, and even the scanning tunneling microscope.

Then what about AI? For decades, the company has been an innovator in this space. As for now, the key to this is the Watson platform. It has become a major revenue generator for IBM.

But AI has still proven challenging. To see how, look at what happened with IBM's moves to leverage AI to diagnose and even treat cancer. This initiative came about in 2011, after Watson stunned the world when it beat the top *Jeopardy!* champions.

At first, there was lots of momentum and excitement. IBM had little problem signing up marquee customers.

Unfortunately, Watson was not up to the task. There was essentially little progress, despite the billions spent. There were even cases where the AI algorithms made things worse, such as with coming up with inaccurate outcomes. As a result, customers started to back off and cancel contracts (this is according to a story in *The Wall Street Journal*).[13]

Then again, a particularly tough issue about cancer is that it is much more than just about analyzing medical information. There is also a need to understand environmental factors and genetics. The complexities can be mind boggling.

All in all, it was a stark example of the limits of AI. There is still much to be done to make it powerful.

IBM's story also provides a lesson on how to temper expectations. When you try to "boil the ocean," you can be setting yourself up for failure.

Again, as noted earlier in this chapter, a better approach is to be measured. As you learn, you can then get more ambitious.

"Most CEOs are excited about the business potential of artificial intelligence," said Anand Rao, who is the Global AI Lead at PwC. "In fact, PwC's CEO survey finds that 85% of CEOs believe that AI will significantly change the way they do business within the next five years. But the first step for many organizations will be to focus on practical AI, or as I like to call it, 'boring AI.' This approach will set businesses up for success with targeted AI projects now, as well as more advanced, comprehensive deployments later. For example, companies can see significant savings from using AI to extract information from tax forms, bills of lading, invoices, and other documents that typically require long and tedious hours of human work. These 'boring AI' projects also provide an opportunity for companies to learn how to implement AI projects: scope the problem, establish a baseline for comparison, label data, train and validate models, and deploy, monitor, and measure the ROI of models. It establishes a solid groundwork for AI implementations in the long run. It can also be used to establish the governance around the responsible use of data and AI, and also serve as a mechanism for organizations to educate their senior management on the advantages and challenges of adopting AI."[14]

Conclusion

As you will see in this book, AI is a journey. And it begins with a clear-cut understanding of the problem to be solved. This will help to focus the organization, increase the odds of success, and allow for the better use of resources. Basically, you do not want to be running science experiments!

---

[13]www.wsj.com/articles/ibm-bet-billions-that-watson-could-improve-cancer-treatment-it-hasnt-worked-1533961147

[14]From the author's interview with Anand Rao on April 19, 2020.

True, the initial target of the project may change. And this is to be expected. There will also be new ideas that pop up for other projects. So it's really critical to keep an open mind and be creative.

In the next chapter, we'll cover the second step in the AI process: putting together the right team.

Key Takeaways

- Success with AI is not about interesting science experiments. Rather, the key is focusing on solving real-world business problems.

- After you identify a problem to be solved, the first step is not necessarily to have a project. A better approach is to first see if your existing applications have AI functions or if there are third-party solutions. The fact is that there are many robust AI applications on the market.

- When evaluating a third-party AI solution, here are some factors to consider: look for strong financial backing, such as from venture capitalists; see if the company has experience in your industry; make sure there are sufficient security and privacy systems; see if the system can be customized; and get an estimate of the ROI.

- Even when a solid third-party AI application is available, a company may still want to do a project anyway. Some reasons are: the technology is highly strategic; there is a need for extensive customization; or there is resistance in putting sensitive data on another company's cloud.

- When looking at a problem to be solved, many times AI is not the right answer. Interestingly enough, there may be a simpler approach available.

- If you decide to create an AI project, you need to explore different areas across the organization that could prove fruitful for transformation. A good way to do this is to set up a workshop with a diverse group (say with technical and non-technical people). There should be a free flowing of ideas and little criticism of them. The goal is idea generation.

- Once you have identified various problems to be solved, start a filtering process. Some factors to consider include: Is there the right kind of data? Is the project focused on a particular area? Is the AI to help with a process that is tedious and repetitive? Is there the right team that is willing to take risks? And what about integrations with legacy systems? Will there need to be extensive work to the foundation to make the AI work?

- After the filtering process, you should come up with one problem to be solved. You can then put together a flow chart for it. This will provide a roadmap for the data scientists. There should also be a timetable for the project.

- The project certainly needs a KPI, which is used to measure success. Often this is about saving hours of employee time. But it could also be to improve customer satisfaction scores, revenues, or risk management.

- It's quite common that a company will retain a consulting firm to help with an AI project. After all, the technology is extremely complex and the failure rate is generally high.

- Some of the benefits of hiring a consulting firm include: you lower the risks and increase the speed of completing the project, which should help your competitive position; you have access to a diverse team with broad skillsets; you can get help with vendor selection and training services; and the firm may also have its own proprietary AI technologies.

- Note that a consulting arrangement can be short term. It can essentially be a way to learn about the process. After this, your own organization can take control of the next projects.

- However, before hiring a consulting firm, it's important to make sure your organization is ready. To do this, you want to identify your data as well as the people who have experience with data science. It is also a good idea to put together a requirements document.

- Consultants usually charge a fixed per-project price or hourly rate, although some may be creative, such as with value-based fees.

- Some of the world's top tech companies have had notable failures with AI. A high-profile case is IBM Watson. The company invested aggressively to use the AI platform to diagnose and treat cancer. But unfortunately, the results proved lacking. It was a stark reminder that, when it comes to AI, it is often best to start with a narrow focus and then learn along the way.

The Team

The main roles for your AI project

The recruitment of AI talent can be a high-stakes game. In some cases, a company may be willing to offer multi-million dollar packages along with significant equity options.

To get a sense of how competitive the environment can be, look at the example of Uber. In 2015, the company was struggling in its efforts to create an autonomous vehicle. The biggest problem: There simply was not enough talented AI engineers on the payroll. The fact is that it was extremely difficult to compete against giants like Apple and Google.

So Uber took a more aggressive approach to recruiting. The company went to Carnegie Mellon University and hired away 40 researchers and scientists. Of course, the school had a distinguished history as an innovator in AI. For example, it was the first to have a degree in machine learning.

Uber had raised $5 billion so there was more than enough resources to offer lucrative pay packages. Let's face it, when it comes to salaries for the academic community, they are far from attractive. Keep in mind that Uber's move was so bold that it garnered headlines in the media.[1]

As should be no surprise, Carnegie Mellon University took a hit. The department saw a reduction in outside funding because it did not have enough resources to execute on the projects.

---

[1] www.wsj.com/articles/is-uber-a-friend-or-foe-of-carnegie-mellon-in-robotics-1433084582

© Tom Taulli 2021

T. Taulli, *Implementing AI Systems*, https://doi.org/10.1007/978-1-4842-6385-3_4

But the Uber episode raised broader concerns. Might Big Tech wield its power to scoop up most of the talent at universities and perhaps stifle creativity and innovation? Aren't academic institutions more willing to explore basic research, which has been critical for cutting-edge developments?

This is all true.

In light of all this, the tech industry saw that there needed to be a better approach. The result was that companies like Facebook, IBM, and Microsoft set up partnerships with universities. There would not only be funding but programs where researchers and scientists could take leaves so as to work for private firms.

It was a reasonable strategy and it has worked fairly well.

But this has certainly not dampened the intense poaching among tech firms! For example, Apple has been particularly aggressive. During the past few years, the company has made the following high-profile hires:

- *John Giannandrea*: Apple recruited him away from Google to become the company's first Senior Vice President of AI. As a sign of the importance of the position, he would report to CEO Tim Cook.

- *Ian Goodfellow*: He was another recruitment from Google by Apple. As the creator of the GAN (Generative Adversarial Network), which we covered in Chapter 2, he was one of the top people in the AI field (he received his PhD at the University of Montreal). At Apple, he took on the role of Director of Machine Learning for the Special Projects Group.[2]

Apple has been hiring academics as well. There was the recruitment of Ruslan Salakhutdinov, a professor at Carnegie Mellon University, to be the Director of AI research.[3] There was also the hiring of Carlos Guestrin, a machine learning expert from the University of Washington.

Oh, and another part of the recruiting process was actually the purchase of startups. These deals have often been referred to as acqui-hires since the main goal is to snag talented engineers. Some of Apple's deals included purchases of Laserlike, Drive.ai, and Fashwell.[4]

---

[2]www.cnbc.com/2019/04/04/apple-hires-ai-expert-ian-goodfellow-from-google.html
[3]www.wsj.com/articles/apple-hires-artificial-intelligence-executive-from-rival-google-1522811544
[4]https://venturebeat.com/2019/12/23/how-the-big-5-bolstered-their-ai-through-acquisitions-in-2019/

Given all this activity, it is certainly tougher for smaller firms or non-tech operators to compete for talent. Yet this should not mean that there is no hope. There are definitely strategies and approaches to building great AI teams.

In this chapter, we'll take a look at these strategies and approaches. But first, let's cover the main roles of an AI team.

The Executive Sponsor

When it comes to implementing new technology, AI is not the only one that has major issues with adoption. All organizations suffer from inertia. Employees get accustomed to certain approaches and processes when it comes to doing their work. When there are attempts to change this, there is often resistance. It's natural. It's almost inevitable.

Regarding AI then, a bottoms-up adoption of the technology is not realistic. There needs to be substantial resources devoted to the effort, in terms of hiring new employees and purchasing new software and systems.

Because of this, an AI project needs an executive sponsor. This is a person who is at a senior level and has the ability to make significant budget decisions. The executive sponsor does not need to be from the tech side, say the CTO. The person can be anyone. But the key is that they have influence in the organization and are willing to take risks.

It's actually common for the executive sponsor to be a head of a department like marketing or sales. The need for AI may arise because there are challenges such as with improving performance or fending off rivals.

However, because of the growing popularity of AI, there still may be bottoms-up activities. And this is OK. This is actually a good sign. It means that adoption may be easier. But then again, an executive sponsor should see this as an opportunity to centralize the initiatives so there is not too much confusion. They will be in a position to set forth the vision and major goals, which will help get the project off to a good start.

"Someone needs to understand what the business is going to do with the insight the AI finds and be a champion for the team," said Pat Ryan, who is the Executive VP of Enterprise Architecture at SPR. "AI teams typically do not produce output for every 'sprint,' like a development team. In many cases, the AI team will spend weeks analyzing, experimenting, and gathering more new data, which could seem to the rest of the organization like they are making little progress. It's the executive sponsor's job to make sure the business understands the value of the team."[5]

---

[5]From the author's interview with Pat Ryan on June 12, 2020.

A recent survey from Deloitte pointed to the critical importance of having an executive sponsor. According to the results, the CEO was actually the lead champion for 29% of the organizations and they were 77% more likely to have exceeded their business goals. They were also 59% more likely to get valuable insights from their models.

Tim Smith, a principal at Deloitte Consulting LLP and the Technology Strategy and Business Transformation Practice Leader, said, "Data science has to permeate company culture starting from the top to see true benefits."[6]

The Project Manager/Business Owner

The executive sponsor does not have the time for day-to-day management of the AI project. In other words, there needs to be a solid project manager or business owner. The focus will be on hitting the goals but also allowing for innovation and new ideas.

The project manager should be a quick study. That is, they need to have a high-level understanding of AI and its capabilities. This will be crucial to effectively communicate with the team, which will involve a mix of technical and non-technical people.

The project manager can be recruited internally. If anything, this may be better since the person will have a good understanding of the business.

In terms of the role of the AI project manager, it is fairly new and continues to evolve. But it is also far from easy. A successful AI project manager must be multi-disciplinary, be willing to keep learning, and be a good listener.

A major part of the role is administrative. There should be clear project plans and timetables. To this end, there are a variety of tools that can help out, such as Asana, SmartSheet, and Monday. They will also help to focus the team and help with the management.

The AI project manager's portfolio will be extensive and will involve the overseeing of data development and cleanup, evaluation of AI tools, help with infrastructure resources, creation and testing of the model, and deployment. But even after this, there is often a need to monitor the models. Over time, they can easily degrade and break down, as the data may be too old or the algorithms not robust enough to handle new conditions. Because of this, as more models are deployed, the management requirements can get quite complicated.

---

[6]www2.deloitte.com/us/en/pages/about-deloitte/articles/press-releases/deloitte-survey-analytics-and-ai-driven-enterprises-thrive.html

Something else: An AI project manager will have to work across different departments within the organization, say IT, legal, marketing, sales, and so on. They will also need to be able to communicate with executives in order to keep up the momentum for the project. Maintaining the buy-in will be crucial in handling bottlenecks and politics.

As for managing the AI team, the project manager will have the challenge of working with technical and non-technical employees. This means having, at times, to mediate issues and fights.

Even when a project manager is able to facilitate a project, there is the problem that AI often involves much trial-and-error. So in the early stages, it is likely that there will be failure, which can hurt the morale of the team and cause concern with the executives. This is why it is essential that everyone understands that AI is never smooth. It takes discipline and patience.

Then what type of background to look for in an AI project manager? You definitely want someone who has experience working on major projects where there were notable risks and a need for multi-tasking. Now this does not necessarily have to be a tech effort, but it helps. For example, it is common for AI project managers to have experience with software development projects. Another thing that is critical is that they have good business writing skills, with an ability to make complex topics understandable. The role will involve lots of emails and Slack communications!

The Subject Matter Expert

The SME (subject matter expert) is someone who has a strong understanding of a particular domain. For example, they may be the person who knows a process in the company, say for invoices or how to process a claim. Or the SME could have a background on how to deal with customers in an industry.

In relation to an AI project, you can usually find the SME within the organization, although in some cases there may be a need to get a consultant. So if you are looking to rethink a company process, you might want to have someone with a background in a methodology framework like Six Sigma or lean. They will also bring a fresh perspective to the process.

The SME will help with evaluating the types of data needed. They will also work with a data scientist to craft the model. And then the SME will provide assistance in evaluating the results.

In some circumstances, the hiring of an SME can be creative. Just look at Intuit. When the company built its conversational AI bot for QuickBooks, it recruited Scott Ganz as the Principal Content Designer. His background? He was actually a screenwriter! He won an Emmy for his work on *Wordgirl*.

His role has been to work with the engineering and design teams to develop a personality for the AI system. For the most part, the focus has been more than just understanding the customer but getting a sense of the underlying emotions. This is certainly critical when it comes to sensitive issues like money.

Ganz has also been helpful in simplifying the user experience. For example, instead of the bot talking about "accounts receivable," it mentions "who owes me money?"[7]

The Business Analyst

A business analyst is someone who uses data analysis to help improve the operations of a company. Such a person usually has a business degree or MBA, with a background in using BI (Business Intelligence) tools such as Tableau, MicroStrategy, and SAS. There are also a variety of certifications for business analysts: PMI Professional in Business Analysis (PBA), IIBA Certification of Competency in Business Analysis (CCBA), and IQBBA Certified Foundation Level Business Analyst (CFLBA).

Some of the common tasks include creating financial models, say to forecast sales or churn. They may also look at analysis to help reduce costs or to improve pricing. A business analyst will then create reports or dashboards, which are presented to executives and managers.

Then what would the role be for an AI project? It could actually be significant. After all, many projects are focused on rethinking processes or lowering costs. What's more, a business analyst can find and evaluate data sources. There could also be integrations with the BI systems.

Because a business analyst will have analytics skills, they could be a good candidate to ultimately transition to the role of a data scientist. Or, as is becoming more common, a business analyst could become a "citizen data scientist." That is, the person does not have the usual qualifications but can still perform a variety of tasks of a data scientist.

The Data Engineer

A data engineer will help create reliable data pipelines, such as with cloud databases and data warehouses. This process will often involve extensive wrangling of the data sets like deduplication, handling missing items, finding anomalies and outliers, and even detecting potential bias.

---

[7]www.forbes.com/sites/tomtaulli/2019/08/30/how-screenwriting-can-boost-ai-artificial-intelligence/#a3eff56586aa

When looking for a data engineer, you want someone who knows Python, R, and SQL. In terms of the educational background, it is usually a Bachelor's or Master's in statistics, mathematics, or computer science. They should also have experience with the following:

- Workflow engines such as Azure Data Factor, Airflow, Google Cloud Composer, and so on

- Data modelling

- ETL (extract, transform, load) design, implementation, and maintenance (this is a process for data integration, usually for a data warehouse)

- Querying of databases like Spark, Hive, Presto, Hadoop, and so on

- GIT version control

- A/B testing

The data engineer will usually work closely with the data scientists. They will not only present the data sets, in a good form, but also provide input for the modelling and testing.

The Data Scientist

The data scientist, who may also be called an AI engineer, is the person who develops the AI models. No doubt, this person often gets much of the attention. But they will still rely on a team of other important people. Perhaps there are some unicorn data scientists, but they are very rare!

■ **Note** There's an old joke: A data scientist is someone who knows more about statistics than a computer scientist and more computer science than a statistician. OK, this is not too funny! But this does point out that a data scientist has a blend of unique technical skills.

A data scientist will have a range of knowledge and capabilities that includes traditional statistics, probability, and decision theory. And yes, they should have a background in understanding machine learning, deep learning, and perhaps NLP. But a good data scientist will also have an understanding of basic business principles. This is essential since they will work with a myriad of stakeholders like those in marketing, sales, finance, and legal.

Their educational background is usually quite extensive. For example, it is common for a data scientist to have a PhD or Master's degree in computer science or machine learning. They will also have experience with academic theories and programming languages like Java, C, C++, Scala, and Python. They will then have to know AI platforms such as TensorFlow, Keras, scikit-learn, Caffe, and PyTorch, as well as cloud systems like AWS, Azure, and Databricks.

The Designer

Even if an AI model works, has accurate results, and provides useful insights, this may not be enough. Consider that the end user is often someone who is not technical. So if the AI model has a complex UI (user interface) or UX (user experience), then there may be little adoption. The result would be a waste of resources, and the AI initiative may ultimately be abandoned.

To avoid this, you can have a designer put together a compelling AI application. This could involve a simplified menu, effective graphics, and helpful visualizations.

A designer does not necessarily have to be a full-time person. It is actually more common to have this person involved on a contractor basis.

AI Tester

AI models can be temperamental. Even slight changes can have wide variances in the outcomes. While a data scientist can provide some level of testing, there should still be someone else to lead this role. This person is known as the AI tester or quality assurance engineer.

They will spend much time creating test plans and cases to run against the models. Often these plans will involve automated scripts. The AI tester will also manage the bug tracking process.

There are a variety of testing tools available, such as Selenium, Eggplant, WebTest, Mercury QTP, or Watir. They can help streamline the process but also facilitate the different approaches, such as the following:

- *Black box testing*: In this situation, the tester does not know the structure of the application. Rather, they put together a variety of inputs and test cases for the evaluation.

- *White box testing*: In this case, the tester has access to the underlying code and data sets. This allows for helping to detect security exposures or poor structure.

- *Grey box testing*: This is a blend of the black and white box testing approaches.

Then which one to use? Given the complexities of AI, the grey box testing approach may be the best. This will provide for comprehensive testing.

An AI tester can also be helpful in evaluating the user interface, although it is advisable to have many people in the organization to also test this and to ask for feedback.

As for the background for an AI tester, they will usually have a BS in computer science or a related engineering field. They will also have experience with a language like Python and shell scripting languages.

The AI Solution Architect

Even startups have complicated IT environments and legacy systems. This can present challenges when implementing AI within an organization.

To help with this, there is the AI solution architect. The main role of this person is to integrate the AI within the IT infrastructure. If done right, this can help accelerate the implementation process but also help with the scaling.

The AI solution architect will need a familiarity with the core concepts of machine learning as well as the frameworks. They should also have experience with CRMs, ERPs, and middleware systems. Furthermore, a background with GPUs and modern architectures like Kubernetes is a plus.

And as for education, they will usually have a graduate degree in a field like computer science, machine learning, statistics, or mathematics.

Machine Learning Engineer

A machine learning engineer is involved in the process of machine learning operations or MLOps. The main focus is turning the AI into a product and maintaining the effectiveness of the models. Consider that, over time, models usually drift. So a machine learning engineer will monitor this and make the necessary adjustments.

This person will have experience in quickly prototyping new models but also placing them in production, such as in Python or R. They should have a background with handling big data pipelines as well.

Regarding education, a machine learning engineer will usually have a graduate degree in computer science, statistics, engineering, or mathematics.

Recruiting

Elon Musk is one of the world's best recruiters of tech talent. Tesla has over 48,000 employees and many of them have deep technical backgrounds.

AI is also a key to the company's growth strategy. All the cars have the hardware capabilities for autonomous driving, such as surround cameras, ultrasonic sensors, forward-facing radar, and AI chips. These systems are updated via the cloud.

In terms of recruiting, Musk has unconventional approaches. In fact, this is a necessity because of the talent shortages across the world.

Musk will even go to Twitter for his recruiting efforts. Here are some examples:

- "At Tesla, using AI to solve self-driving isn't just icing on the cake, it the cake" - @lexfridman

- Join AI at Tesla! It reports directly to me & we meet/email/text almost every day. My actions, not just words, show how critically I view (benign) AI. https://www.tesla.com/autopilotAI

- Tesla will hold a super fun AI party/hackathon at my house with the Tesla AI/autopilot team in about four weeks. Invitations going out soon.

All this certainly points to how Musk sees AI as a strategic priority. He has also been effective in creating a vision for his company that is quite compelling to engineers and researchers. While compensation is certainly important, people also want to work for a company that has a purpose.

In job listings for AI, here's what Tesla notes: "As a software engineer on the Autopilot Computer Vision and AI team, you will contribute to one of the most advanced and widely-deployed computer vision stacks in the world. Along with top researchers from academia and some of the most experienced autonomous vehicle engineers in the industry, you will marry cutting-edge deep learning algorithms with robust, real-time software, and deliver safety-critical features to hundreds of thousands of customers. You will develop and support a host of different projects, driven first-and-foremost by our mission to deploy the safest and most effective product in the market."[8]

---

[8]https://bit.ly/3fMxg95

The ad goes on to say that a person needs a "MS or PhD in Computer Science, Physics, Electrical Engineering or proof of exceptional skills in related fields, with practical software engineering experience." In other words, you do not have to have a formal education in the area, so long as you have "practical" experience.

This is by design. In an interview with a German auto magazine, Musk said: "There's no need even to have a college degree at all, or even high school."[9]

He also looks for talent in disciplines like physics, social sciences, and mathematics. Such people not only have quantitative skills but also bring diverse ideas to the team.

Again, when it comes to recruiting AI talent, you need to be very creative. Granted, this is not to say traditional approaches should be shunned. Using technical recruiters is definitely good to do, as long as they have strong AI skills.

You should also leverage online resources like job sites, forums, online communities (like Hackernews.com and AngelList), and LinkedIn. Recruiting AI talent usually takes a lot of courting and patience.

Reskilling

Reskilling or upskilling is when you train existing employees to transition to becoming part of the AI technical team. This is becoming easier as there are a myriad of online courses such as from Coursera, Udacity, open.ai, and deeplearning.ai as well as bootcamps. More traditional universities are also offering executive programs for AI and data science.

■ **Note**   In February 2020, Udacity launched an online learning executive program called AI For Business Leaders, in partnership with BMW. It has quickly become one of the most popular courses on the platform. The goal is to teach technical AI concepts to business leaders quickly. A typical course takes about four to eight weeks to complete.

An example of a successful reskilling program is from Bloomberg, which is the dominant data platform for the financial industry. The company has invested significantly in AI and machine learning to enhance its products and services. There are more than 150 data scientists, researchers, and engineers on the Data Science Team, which is part of the CTO's office and AI Group. Some of

---

[9]www.cnbc.com/2020/02/03/elon-musk-is-recruiting-for-tesla-education-is-irrelevant.html

the innovations have included: using models to predict the impact of news events on stock prices, sentiment analysis based on social media, product recommendation systems, and anomaly detection for large time series data sets.

Back in 2017, Bloomberg realized that it could not rely solely on traditional recruiting for its AI efforts. So the company launched its own educational program. It covers the core concepts of AI and how the technology applies to Bloomberg systems. Over time, the company has developed nine courses.

Interestingly enough, during the summer of 2018, Bloomberg made public 30 training videos. You can find them here: `https://bloomberg.github.io/foml/#lectures`. Some of the topics include an introduction to statistical theory, stochastic gradient descent, black box machine learning, loss functions for regression and classification, and support vector machines.

Why did Bloomberg do this? First of all, it was a way to provide a resource to its own client base. Next, the videos are a statement of Bloomberg's commitment to its own investment in learning, which has been useful in recruiting talent.

True, not all companies have the resources to do this. But then again, there should still be some investment in education, both for reskilling and existing AI employees. This is vital for success.

However, education is still not enough. There needs to be initiatives to provide employees ways to implement their new skills. In the meantime, an organization needs to give incentives for mentoring.

Oh, and the training should not just be for technical talent. It's a good idea to provide beginner level training for all employees. This will go a long way in creating a data-driven culture.

Regarding the process of reskilling, one effective approach is to first identify those employees who have backgrounds with similarities to AI. For example, a conventional full stack or backend software engineer can learn to become a data engineer on the job and with modest training. The same goes for a business analyst.

■ **Note** A survey from Deloitte points out that when all employees have been trained on analytics, about 88% exceeded their objectives. This is compared to 61% that did not.[10]

---

[10]`www2.deloitte.com/us/en/insights/topics/analytics/insight-driven-organization.html`

Team Size

Even if you have a large budget, it is not realistic to assemble a full-blown AI team quickly. The market is just too competitive. So in the early phases, you need to focus on some of the key players. For example, it is usually advisable to spend top dollar on a qualified data scientist. This person will not only help with crafting effective models but could provide assistance with reskilling and recruiting. After all, he or she likely will have a strong network.

It's often a good idea to keep the team small anyway. This should allow for more agility. This is consistent with the so-called two-pizza rule, which is what Amazon's CEO and founder Jeff Bezos instituted at his company in the early days. This is where an internal team would have no more people than two pizzas can feed!

Salary Size

As AI has grown in popularity, the salaries have likewise seen growth. The main reason is that there has been an ongoing shortage of people with the necessary technical skills and experience in the space.

The job site Indeed put together a survey on AI salaries that was based on over 78,000 employees (as of the summer of 2020).[11] Here's what it found (salaries per year):

- Machine Learning Engineer - $140,686
- Software Engineer - $109,321
- Research Scientist - $98,788
- Data Scientist - $122,788
- Scientist - $101,628
- Senior Software Engineer - $132,367
- Research Engineer - $94,910
- Software Engineer Intern - $76,579

But this likely understates greatly the compensation. Many AI employees work for technology companies that provide stock options and other forms of equity incentives. The result is that the compensation could easily be two to three times as much as the salary.

---

[11]www.indeed.com/salaries/artificial-intelligence-Salaries

In the Indeed survey, there was a 5.8% increase in 2019 for average AI salaries. This is compared to an average of 2.9% for all categories. The survey also reported a 15% increase in searches for AI candidates.

Chief AI Officer

Generally, it's the Chief Technology Officer (CTO), the Chief Information Officer (CIO), or the Chief Information Security Officer (CISO) who is the high-level executive who oversees AI initiatives. But as the technology becomes more strategic, some companies have created a new role, such as the Chief AI Officer (CAIO) or the Chief Algorithms Officer (CAO).

This role will often involve someone with a PhD in data science or machine learning. That is, they can read the academic papers and keep up with the latest developments in AI. But this background in academia can also be helpful in recruiting. What's more, a CAIO should have a business background, such as with understanding how to implement complex systems successfully.

One of the most notable CAIO's is Yann LeCun (he has over 203,000 followers on Twitter), who is an executive at Facebook (the company refers to his position as VP and Chief AI Scientist). In 1987, he received his PhD in Computer Science from the Universite Pierre et Marie Curie in Paris, France, and then worked at AT&T's Bell Labs. He developed optical character recognition technologies for interpreting checks and created DjVu, which allowed for image compression for websites.

In 2003, he became a professor at NYU and founded the NYU Center for Data Science. During his academic career, he published over 180 technical papers on topics like AI, machine learning, computer vision, and computational neuroscience. When he joined Facebook in 2013, he maintained his professor role on a part-time basis.[12]

In 2019, he shared the Turing Award with Yoshua Bengio and Geoffrey Hinton. They are often called the Godfathers of AI.[13]

Conclusion

As you've seen in this chapter, there are many different roles for an AI team. This is why it is incredibly important for there to be strong collaboration. And because of the inherent complexities of AI, it's essential that the process be iterative. If the pace gets rushed, then failure can be the result.

---

[12]http://yann.lecun.com/ex/bio.html
[13]www.theverge.com/2019/3/27/18280665/ai-godfathers-turing-award-2018-yoshua-bengio-geoffrey-hinton-yann-lecun

In the next chapter, we'll take a look at the data process.

Key Takeaways

- An AI team involves many roles. Here's a look at the main ones:

    - *Executive sponsor*: This is a person from the executive suite who champions the AI project. This role is critical since there often needs to be substantial resources, especially for hiring technical talent and purchasing software. But the executive sponsor does not have to be the CIO or CTO. Rather, they should be someone who has the ability to galvanize the organization and has the right budget authority.

    - *Project manager/business owner*: This is the person who takes on the day-to-day management of the project. The focus will be on helping to set and hit the goals. The project manager can be recruited internally, but they should have some technical skillsets.

    - *SME (subject matter expert)*: As the name implies, this is a person who has a strong understanding of a particular domain or area of the company, such as its processes or customer base. Usually the SME is recruited internally.

    - *Business analyst*: This person uses data analysis to help improve the operations of a company. They create models, reports, and dashboards with BI tools. Regarding an AI project, a business analyst can understand business processes, evaluate data, and integrate systems.

    - *Data engineer*: This person will find the right data sources and structure them properly, such as with fixing duplications and missing items.

    - *Data scientist (or AI engineer)*: This is the person who creates the AI models. They certainly have a strong background in statistics, machine learning, and deep learning but also some background in business.

    - *Designer*: A designer can create better interfaces, which should lead to improved adoption of the AI. A designer is usually a part-time position.

- *AI tester*: This person focuses on trying to find problems with AI models.

- *AI solution architect*: This person handles the integration of the AI with the IT infrastructure. They can also set up the systems to help scale the technology.

- *Machine learning engineer*: This person is responsible for turning the AI into a product. The role also involves tracking and evaluating the models.

- Recruiting AI talent is far from easy. It's something that is ongoing. Because of the shortage for tech talent, it is usually necessary to find people who may not necessarily have direct AI experience. For example, they may have advanced degrees in physics and mathematics. Thus, the process should be easier for training them in machine learning and deep learning.

- Reskilling and upskilling are also very effective. They can be a way to build a strong AI team. This approach is also getting much easier because of the proliferation of online courses, bootcamps, and executive degree programs.

- Even if you have a big budget, this does not mean you should be aggressive in hiring AI talent. This can lead to major problems. The process should not be rushed. Actually, small teams are often better.

- As AI has become more important, there has emerged a new role at the executive level: the Chief AI Officer or CAIO. This person usually has a strong background in AI, such as a PhD. They should be able to explain complex topics to the rest of the C-suite.

Data Preparation

The fuel for AI

In late 2015, IBM announced the acquisition of the Weather Company—which included the weather data, forecast information, website, app, and various intellectual property. The price tag was over an estimated $2 billion.[1]

What was the rationale for this? Was IBM getting into the weather business?

The deal was actually great for the company. Data is the fuel for AI, and weather data has broad applications. IBM folded the Weather Company assets into the Watson AI platform. The forecasting segment, called WSI, was likely the most important asset. The business included license revenue from over 5,000 companies in industries like airlines and utilities.

In terms of the data assets, they included three billion weather forecast reference points. There was also infrastructure for data collection from over 40 million smartphones and 50,000 airplane flights per day.

IBM was not the only mega tech suitor that was interested. Google had already made a bid for the Weather Company but it was rebuffed. It's also important to note that IBM had a partnership with the company.

---

[1] www.wsj.com/articles/ibm-to-buy-weather-co-s-digital-data-assets-1446039939

© Tom Taulli 2021
T. Taulli, *Implementing AI Systems*, https://doi.org/10.1007/978-1-4842-6385-3_5

Here's what John Kelly, the Senior Vice President at IBM Solutions Portfolio and Research, said about the deal: "The Weather Company's extremely high-volume data platform, coupled with IBM's global cloud and the advanced cognitive computing capabilities of Watson, will be unsurpassed in the Internet of Things, providing our clients significant competitive advantage as they link their business and sensor data with weather and other pertinent information in real time. This powerful cloud platform will position IBM to arm entire industries with deep multimodal insights that will help enterprises gain clarity and take action from the oceans of data being generated around them."[2]

Here are some of the ways weather data and IoT can be combined for powerful results:

- Models can use data from social media sentiment and transformation flows to help retailers and distributors improve their supply chains.

- Weather data can help airlines save millions of dollars with lower fuel consumption, reduced delays, and less airport congestion.

But the acquisition of the Weather Company was not the only deal. IBM had already struck arrangements with companies like Twitter, Apple, Medtronic, and Johnson & Johnson for data sources. There was also the $700 million purchase of Merge Health, which owned a large dataset.

These moves from IBM highlight the strategic importance of data for AI. It's also a key reason why data-rich companies like Netflix, Google, Facebook, and Microsoft are leaders in the industry.

In this chapter, we will take a look at data and how to use it effectively for an AI project.

The Data Explosion

The growth of data is staggering. Based on research from IDC, more than 59 zettabytes of data will be created in 2020 and the growth will be 26% per year until 2024 (a zettabyte is 1,000,000,000,000,000,000,000 bytes).[3] To put things into perspective, the next three years will have about the same amount of data as the past 30! IDC actually increased its forecast because of the impact of the COVID-19 virus as there was an acceleration of the usage of

---

[2]https://business.weather.com/news/ibm-plans-to-acquire-the-weather-companys-product-and-technology-businesses-extends-power-of-watson-to-the-internet-of-things
[3]www.datanami.com/2020/05/19/global-datasphere-to-hit-59-zettabytes-in-2020-alone-idc-projects/

work-from-home technologies, which rely heavily on data-intensive video streaming. But another factor is the significant increases in metadata and sensor data, such as for the Internet of Things.

When boiling things down, there are four main types of data. They include the following:

- *Structured data*: This is the data that is stored in relational databases and spreadsheets. Because there is usually labeling, this type of data is fairly easy to work with. There are a myriad of BI (business intelligence) tools that can glean insights or create visualizations from this information. And yes, when working with an AI model, structured data certainly makes the process much easier. But the reality is that there is usually not enough of this data. The rule of thumb is that about 20% of datasets are structured.

- *Unstructured data*: This is the majority of the information available for AI models. Examples of unstructured data include images, emails, videos, text files, satellite images, and social media messages. In terms of storage, there are next-generation systems like NoSQL databases that can better handle this type of information. But when it comes to AI models, one of the biggest challenges is finding ways to prepare and analyze unstructured data.

- *Semi-structured data*: As the name implies, this is a blend of structured and unstructured data. In a dataset, the majority of the items are usually unstructured. An example of semi-structured data is XML (Extensible Markup Language), which maps information on a document using techniques like JSON (JavaScript Object Notation). This helps to facilitate the exchange of information using APIs (application programming interfaces).

- *Time-series data*: This can be either structured or unstructured. But for the most part, time-series data involves interactions, like the "customer journey" on the Web and mobile devices. This type of data has become much more important for AI models, especially with the growth of the IoT.

With the growth in data, there has emerged the megatrend of big data. Gartner analyst Doug Laney coined this term in 2001 and it caught the attention of the corporate world. There were even startups that began to call themselves big data providers and many of them were able to raise substantial amounts of venture capital.

According to Laney, big data has three key attributes: volume, variety, and velocity. They are known as the three Vs.

Let's take a look at each:

- *Volume*: This is about the enormous scale of the data, which is usually unstructured. There is no bright-line definition for the amount, but the volume probably is in the tens of terabytes. In the early days of big data, the handling of large amounts of data was a major challenge. Yet with the innovations in cloud computing, the process has become much easier.

- *Variety*: This is the diversity of the data, which is a blend of structured, semi-structured, and unstructured data. There is a diversity of sources and uses, say from IoT, social media, and so on.

- *Velocity*: This is the speed at which the data is generated. The sources are often the mega tech platforms like YouTube, Facebook, and Salesforce.com. They create enormous amounts of data (often this is user-generated). To allow for this, these companies invest significant amounts in building data centers across the world (this is often a major topic on earnings calls for Wall Street). When it comes to the three Vs, velocity is usually the most challenging.

After Laney came up with his framework, more Vs have been created. This is an indication of the growth and complexity of big data. Here are some of the other Vs:

- *Visualization*: This involves the creation of graphs and charts to better understand data.

- *Value*: This is about the usefulness or effectiveness of the data. Generally, this means that the data needs to come from a trusted source.

- *Variability*: This describes the inevitable change of data over time. This is particularly the case with channels like social media.

- *Veracity*: This is the accuracy of the data. Data sets usually have lots of problems and there needs to be much wrangling.

The bottom line: Big data is a big topic! And yes, it is constantly evolving. But this category is essential for having a strong AI project.

The Database Market

In the early 1960s, corporations started to look at mainframe computers as an effective way to manage operations like payroll and financials. But the computer languages were too complicated for non-technical people and did not handle the kinds of functions that businesses needed, such as with currencies and reporting. This is why COBOL (Common Business Oriented Language) was created. The language had English-like commands as well as the ability to ingest large amounts of data. The use of the COBOL language would even lead to the development of databases, which helped to power platforms like SABRE, which allowed American Airlines to manage reservations.

Yet the database technology remained quite rudimentary for quite a while. The system was based usually on batch processing since access to the data was from tape storage.

But in 1970, an innovation emerged that would transform the database market. This came from an IBM computer scientist, Edger Codd, who published a paper called "A Relational Model of Data for Large Shared Data Banks." In it, he set forth the fundamentals of the relational database. At the heart of this was an easy scripting language called SQL or Structured Query Language. It included English-like commands to do CRUD (create, read, update, and delete) operations. This was possible because the relational database was organized into various tables that had connections to each other with primary and foreign keys.

The main relationships include

- *One-to-one*: The is where a row in a table is linked to one row in another table. An example of this is a driver's license, which is a unique number that can allow for a unique reference to a customer.

- *One-to-many*: This is a relationship in which one row in a table is linked to two or more other tables. For example, a table for customers could link to various tables that have purchase orders.

- *Many-to-many*: This is a fairly complex relationship, where more than one table is linked to more than two other tables. This is the case when multiple reports have different authors.

With these types of relationships, it was possible to create highly sophisticated database systems. But interestingly enough, Codd's innovation did not get much attention. IBM did not even think it had much potential! The company believed that relational databases were not scalable for mission-critical corporate environments. Instead, IBM continued to focus on its proprietary database technologies—and this would prove to be a huge mistake.

Instead, it was entrepreneur Larry Ellison who saw the advantages of relational databases and he formed a company called Oracle in 1977 to capitalize on the opportunity. From the start, growth was strong. The emergence of the PC was a major catalyst. Computers were no longer just for large enterprises. Even small businesses saw the benefits of this technology.

The database industry would see a myriad of startups pop up, such as Sybase, Ashton-Tate, Paradox, and FoxPro. But by the end of the 1980s, Oracle would be the dominate player in the industry and this continues today. The company's market value is over $170 billion.

Despite this, the relational database is far from perfect. First of all, there is the problem of data sprawl, which is where many different databases proliferate across an organization. Because of this, it can be difficult to centralize the data, say for AI projects.

Next, relational databases were not built for many kinds of modern-day scenarios. That is, they tend to underperform when handling high-velocity data, unstructured data, and cloud platforms. It's also challenging to develop applications on relational databases because the systems can be quite rigid and inflexible.

Something else: Relational databases are not cheap. Not only are the licenses hefty, but there are the ongoing costs for maintenance and upgrades. In a world of big data, a relational database is often uneconomical.

Now this is not to imply that relational databases are dinosaurs. The technology will remain a major part of the IT world. But new approaches have emerged, such as NoSQL and cloud-based databases, which we will cover next.

Next-Generation Databases

Until the late 1990s, much of the development for databases came from large software vendors. They had the resources, engineers, and customer bases to be successful. When it comes to databases, customers want a vendor with a strong foundation.

But there was a problem: the database software vendors were not innovating enough. As a result, programmers started to develop their own open source projects. With the rapid growth of the Internet, it was becoming possible to get quick and wide distribution for software. This would be a game changer for the database market.

A big part of the development was for data warehouses, which can store huge amounts of information. This technology got much attention because of the rise of large Internet platforms.

One of the pioneers of open source data warehouses is Doug Cutting. First he created Lucene, which was a sophisticated text searching application. But as usage increased significantly, he realized he needed a better database infrastructure. This led him to develop Hadoop with Mike Cafarella. Cutting based Hadoop on a paper he read from Google that set forth the framework for a massive file system. He expanded on this greatly and developed MapReduce, which made it possible to process huge amounts of data across various services. The system would then merge these to allow for the creation of reports.

As should be no surprise, the early adopters of Hadoop were companies like Yahoo!, Facebook, and Twitter. They had an urgent need for better ways to handle the firehouse of data on their platforms. And for the most part, Hadoop was an effective solution. The technology made it easier for these companies to run analytics across their datasets so as to improve user engagement.

Yet Hadoop had its limitations. Venture-backed startups like Hortonworks would see this as an opportunity to build systems such as YARN on the Hadoop platform. This allowed for enterprise-level features like online data, interactive SQL, and in-memory processing. The upshot was that Hadoop saw rapid adoption across the corporate world.

Of course other open source data warehouse projects emerged. One of the most popular turned out to be Apache Spark, which has become especially useful for AI. This system deals with the limitations of MapReduce by allowing lower latency with the distribution of data.

The founder of the Spark project is Matei Zaharia, who created the technology while at UC Berkeley in 2009. He would go on to launch Databricks, which has raised a whopping $897 million. The company operates a cloud-based platform to work with the Spark system, such as by using Python-like notebooks.

Besides rapid innovation in the data warehouse market, there has also been much change with the structures for databases. This is highlighted with the development of NoSQL systems.

Essentially, this means that the database is non-relational. The data is stored as a free-form document. Some of the key benefits include more flexibility to create sophisticated AI models at massive scale but also to better handle unstructured and semi-structured data. What's more, NoSQL databases generally have lower costs.

By far, the most popular version of this technology is MongoDB. The company was originally a traditional software venture but transitioned to the open source model in 2009. It was certainly the right move. At the time, there was significant demand for innovative databases, such as for smartphone apps and cloud computing.

In late 2017, MongoDB went public in a highly successful IPO, raising $192 million. The valuation was at $1.1 billion. However, within a few years, the market capitalization would hit a hefty $11.4 billion. Since inception, MongoDB has logged more than 110 million downloads and there are over 18,400 customers across more than 100 countries.[4]

Mega tech operators like Amazon.com, Google, Alibaba, and Microsoft have also moved aggressively into the database market, especially with cloud-based offerings. Part of this has been for their internal AI efforts. But these companies also see online databases as a lucrative opportunity.

In the meantime, numerous startups are raising capital to get a piece of the growing market. Perhaps the highest-profile one is Snowflake. Back in 2012, Thierry Cruanes, Benoit Dageville, and Marcin Zukowski co-founded the company. They had experience in the data warehouse industry, having worked at companies like Oracle, IBM, and Google.

Snowflake is a fairly easy system to use. All you need to do is fill out a form to create a sophisticated database. The underlying architecture also is well designed. By separating the storage and compute functions, there is much scaling and the platform is multi-cloud. This is essential for AI applications.

In early 2020, Snowflake raised $479 million at a $12.4 billion valuation from investors like Salesforce.com (NYSE:CRM), Sequoia, Altimeter Capital, and Dragoneer Investment Group. The company would then pull off the biggest software IPO ever, raising 3.4 billion. The market value was at over 67 billion.

Among the cloud-based systems, there has been another interesting technology: the data lake. This allows for ingesting huge databases of structured and unstructured data, which often means little need for reformatting. A data lake is also ideal for AI because they work seamlessly with Apache Spark, TensorFlow, and other analytics platforms.

And finally, there are feature stores, which are databases for hyperscale AI companies like Twitter, Facebook, and Airbnb. This is the most cutting-edge technology for handling data in AI models.

The feature store allows for the storage and processing of enormous amounts of features for AI models. The pioneer of this technology is Uber. In 2015, the company was having severe challenges with the hyper growth. Data was

---

scattered across silos and it was nearly impossible to create useful AI models. So Uber set forth to create a proprietary platform called Michelangelo to streamline and accelerate model creation. The result was that the company was able to develop thousands of models, which helped to greatly improve the app.

The Data Challenge

A study from Anaconda, which included 2,360 data scientists, students, and academics/researchers, found that only about 34% of the time spent on AI is on model selection, training, scoring, and deployment. The rest is about the data. Figure 5-1 is a break-down of this.

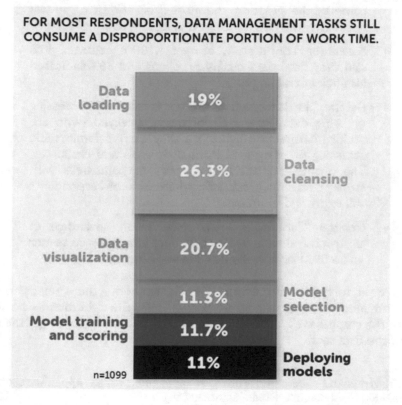

Figure 5-1. In a study from Anaconda, the majority of the time spent on AI is about the data

This may come as a surprise to many, especially business people. After all, the media often focuses on the latest models, such as deep learning. But for these algorithms to have any useful value, there must be high-quality data. And usually huge amounts of it.

Keep in mind that data is often one of the biggest reasons for failed AI models. Consider a report from Appen. It highlights that 40% of executives believe that their organizations do not have enough data or lack the necessary management systems.[5]

Here are some other studies that show issues about data:

- *Gartner:* "Organizations are aware that without sufficient data—or if the situation encountered does not match past data—AI falters. Others know that the more complex the situation, the more likely the situation will not match the AI's existing data, leading to AI failures."[6]

- *Accenture:* From a study of over 1,100 executives, 48% said they have data quality problems and 36% indicated insufficient training data.[7]

- *Deloitte:* "Most executives are not comfortable accessing or using data. Fully 67% of those surveyed (who are senior managers or higher) say they are not comfortable accessing or using data from their tools and resources. The proportion is significant even at companies with strong data-driven cultures, where 37% of respondents still express discomfort."[8]

- *Deloitte:* "Far fewer (18%) have taken advantage of unstructured data (such as product images or customer audio files) or comments from social media."[9]

If you want to have a successful AI implementation, there needs to be a commitment to a strong data strategy. It will build the right foundation. In the rest of the chapter, we'll take a look at some of the strategies to get the most out of the data sets.

---

[5]www.businesswire.com/news/home/20200623005242/en/Appen%E2%80%99s-Annual-State-AI-Report-Finds-Skyrocketing

[6]www.gartner.com/smarterwithgartner/3-barriers-to-ai-adoption/

[7]www.accenture.com/_acnmedia/pdf-73/accenture-strategy-ai-momentum-mind-set-exec-summary-pov.pdf

[8]www2.deloitte.com/us/en/insights/topics/analytics/insight-driven-orga-nization.html

[9]www2.deloitte.com/us/en/insights/topics/analytics/insight-driven-orga-nization.html

Data Collection

The first step in the data process is to see what datasets are available to your organization. This may take some time as data is often spread across different silos. To this end, it's a good idea to talk to managers across different departments. Some of the data sets will be internally created, say from the website, mobile apps, and IoT systems, but there may also be licenses to third-party sources.

But note that there are numerous publicly available data sets that can be extremely useful. For example, governments often provide information for free. There are also sites like Kaggle.com that have plentiful sources.

Interestingly enough, when going through this process, you may miss certain types of data. After all, what about using information from customer surveys? Social media interactions? What about recorded phone calls with customers and prospects? So think expansively when considering data sources.

Even if there is enough data for a model, there could be another issue: corporate politics. Data can be the subject of intense turf wars! This is why it is essential to have an executive sponsor who can deal with these problems.

Data Evaluation

After you have put together your data assets, you can then do some preliminary assessments. This is important because you do not want to spend much time on the data process only to realize that the sources are not good candidates for AI.

First of all, you want to see if the data is relevant. Does it have the kinds of features that will help provide useful outcomes for your model? True, this can be tough to evaluate in the early stages of a project. But an experienced data scientist should be able to come up with a good answer.

Next, is the data timely or is it too old? In some cases, data can become obsolete quickly. If so, you want to make sure you have access to ongoing data streams, or else the model will probably not work.

Another thing to keep in mind is the target audience. Is the population representative? Or is it skewed? For example, if there are a large number of males, then the model may lead to outcomes that are biased.

During the early stages, you also should get a legal review done—that is, does the organization have the right to use the data for the particular purpose of AI? If the information has personally identifiable items, then there may be onerous restrictions or even bans.

Finally, you want to see if your organization has the right IT infrastructure for the data. Can you handle the volumes with your storage systems or data warehouses? If not, what will it take to build such a system? What are the costs?

Data Wrangling

Data wrangling or data preparation is the process of cleaning up, restructuring, and improving a raw data sets. This is an essential step before you can perform an AI model.

"Predictions by a machine learning model are only as good as the data on which the model is based," said Rosaria Silipo, who is a Ph.D. and Principal Data Scientist at KNIME. "And often the data is crap. Missing values, lack of standardization, empty or almost empty attributes, irrelevant attributes, errors in data collection … you name it! Those are all possible causes for low-quality input data. Often, information is in the data; it is just hidden beneath it. Some data cleaning and appropriate data transformation can bring the hidden information up to the surface. The problem in a data lab is that you hire a number of data scientists, and all they want to do is try and tune machine learning models to gain that .01% more in accuracy. Somehow, the data cleaning is the least attractive part in the job description. So, you might think that hiring a data engineer, less specialized than a data scientist, would solve the problem. And this is partially true. However, often it is hard to get data engineers willing to work on data blending and data wrangling tasks who, at the same time, are experts in complex data science scripts. Some help here might come from tools relying on a graphical user interface rather than on scripts, on drag-and-drop rather than on code. The easier the tool, the easier it will be to find data engineers up to the challenge."[10]

An example of a data-wrangling tool is Trifacta, which was launched in 2012. The product grew out of a project from researchers at UC Berkeley and Stanford who wanted to find much better ways to streamline model development.

Trifacta can work in any environment, whether on a desktop, the cloud, or a huge data lake. Here are the key workflows for the platform that mimic what a typical data scientist would use:

---

[10]From the author's interview with Rosaria Silipo on June 12, 2020.

- *Discovery*: This helps explore the usefulness and value of the data for the given project. Trifacta will also detect initial problems, like outliers, and provide a general distribution (such as with visualizations).

- *Structure*: This will help put the data set into a structure that works for models. Note that even well-structured datasets are often not enough.

- *Clean up*: This is the process of dealing with issues like duplications, missing values, and so on. But there is a focus on standardizing the information.

- *Enrichment*: With this, you can augment the data by bringing in other internal data sets or third-party databases. This can be complicated, requiring joins, unions, and other derivations.

- *Validation*: This tests the data for consistency and quality. The system also handles values across multiple dimensions.

- *Publishing*: This provides for the delivery of the data, such as loading it into certain analytics packages or even archiving it.

A case study of Trifacta is GlaxoSmithKline, which is a leading pharmaceutical company that has operations in more than 150 countries. It conducts large numbers of clinical trials that require sophisticated data management, such as with the preparation, collection, and distribution.

But one of the issues is searching for data, which is extremely complex. Using the traditional approach, the process could take weeks to months. So GlaxoSmithKline was missing out on opportunities for innovation.

With Trifacta, the company was able to allow clinical researchers to do their own wrangling of the R&D data, and this greatly reduced the turnaround times. A big part of this was allowing for rich visualizations.

But data searching and exploration are not the only benefits. Going forward, GlaxoSmithKline will be in a much better position to use the information to build advanced AI models. This should further accelerate the drug development process and provide for new discoveries.

However, data tools like Trifacta cannot do everything. There is still a need to have some level of human intervention in the data wrangling process.

So then, here are some of the common techniques:

- *Outliers*: This is where some data is significantly outside the general range of the distribution. This could mean that some of the items are really not representative or there could be errors. Then again, there are scenarios where you actively look for outliers, such as for fraud detection (which involves low-probability events).

- *Standardization*: Data may have inconsistent formats. For example, "California" may be abbreviated as "CA." For purposes of a model, this can degrade the outcome. This is why there should be standardization for how data is expressed or labeled.

- *Duplications*: This is common with data sets. And yes, you want to root them out.

- *Creation*: With a certain data type, you can create a new one. For example, if you have dates of births, you can calculate the ages by subtracting the years from the current year.

- *Conversation table*: This is a system that translates data from one standard to another. An example is where you have information expressed in the decimal system and you want to convert it to the metric system.

- *Binning*: You may not necessarily need to be too granular for the data. Hey, is it really important whether a person is 25 or 27? In most cases, the answer is no. Instead, you can group the data with ranges, such as between 20 to 40 and so on.

- *One-hot encoding*: To see how this works, let's take an example. Suppose you have a data set that has three types of iPhones: iPhone 11 Pro, iPhone 11, and iPhone SE. You could convert them into numbers, where iPhone 11 Pro is 1, iPhone SE is 2, and so on. But when this is processed in a model, the AI may consider iPhone SE better because it has a higher number! But with one-hot encoding, you can come up with a neutral classification system, such as is_iPhone11Pro, is_iPhone11, and is_iPhoneSE. Thus, for each row of data, you would put 1 for the phone that is in use and 0 for the rest.

- *Validation rules*: You can put rules in places to improve the quality of the data. For example, if an age is a negative number, it can be flagged.

- *Missing data*: One approach is to use an average for this. True, it is not perfect, but it can help smooth out some of the gaps. Although, if there is a large amount of missing data, it might be advisable to not use this information.

Data Labeling

Creating labels for data, which is known as data annotation, is often required because the raw data set is not in a workable form.

"Labeling the data consistently at scale can be both a technological and business challenge," said Alyssa Simpson Rochwerger, who is the VP of AI and Data at Appen. "Labeling large volumes of high-quality data can be expensive, and it's easy to spend a lot of money and get back bad data. It's easy to label 100 or 1,000 examples, but it's an entirely different matter to label 100k or 1M or 100M items to achieve the accuracy and precision a business use case requires. Take, for example, a large financial services company we work with that builds a product that allows you to take a picture of a receipt and 'magically' it is transcribed and uploaded into the expense software. Behind the scenes, that requires lots of humans to transcribe receipts since the AI model requires such high precision. Can you imagine if there was a mistake? The company would look silly! Right now, they have built a model that allows for them to send 10% of the data to a model with high confidence, and they are expanding that over time using high quality training data."[11]

However, the data labeling is not a "set and forget it" process. There usually needs to be ongoing refreshing in order to have success with the models. "It's not enough to gather and label training data at one point in time and never come back to it," said Rochwerger. "It's critical to think through a constant feedback loop and training data pipeline to measure the performance of the model over time as well as retrain and address low accuracy or low performant areas. For my example about receipts, when the expense product first launched, the team only took into consideration US-based receipts as in US dollars, with the date format in the US and English language. However, some customers were uploading receipts from international business trips and the product could not handle those use cases."

As you saw earlier in this book, companies like Facebook have used semi-structured data, like tags on Instagram, to help accelerate the process. But unfortunately, this is usually not an option for most data sets.

Even if the data set is manageable, you still may not want to do the labeling in-house. Keep in mind that this process can be intricate and complicated. You will likely need to purchase some software tools but also have some people

---

[11]From the author's interview with Alyssa Simpson Rochwerger on June 5, 2020.

for quality assurance. If you do not set things up properly, the data could easily be corrupted.

Another option is to use a crowdsourcing option, which can certainly be effective. With this approach, you will specify how you want the data set labeled and then the third-party provider will recruit the people for the project.

One of the top labeling outsourcers is Appen. The company has actually been around since 1996 and is publicly traded on the Australian stock exchange. During 2019, revenues jumped by 47% to $536 million and adjusted earnings came to $101 million. This is a clear sign that the data labeling industry is seeing tremendous growth.

For its training data services, Appen has more than one million contractors in more than 130 countries who speak 180 languages and dialects. But Appen also has created its own AI platform that helps to automate the data labeling process, which is built for quality, accuracy, and speed.

For a case study of a customer, take a look at Zefr. The company develops technology for YouTube ad targeting and has customers like Target, Netflix, Adidas, and Honda.

But when Zefr internally crowdsourced the data labeling, it could only handle about 15,000 videos per month. This was simply not enough for the scale of Zefr. By using Appen's contractors, the company was able to increase the output to about 100,000 per month. Because of this, Zefr was able to have much richer and effective data to train models for more accurate video recommendations.

"For data labeling, human-in-the-loop training data provides the highest quality," said Wilson Pang, who is the Chief Technology Officer at Appen. "People involved in the labeling, training, testing, and tuning will ensure a higher rate of accuracy and success of a project."[12]

■ **Note** According to a study from research firm Cognilytica, the market for outsourcing data labeling is expected to go from $150 million in 2018 to $1 billion by 2023.[13]

---

[12]From the author's interview with Wilson Pang on June 2, 2020.
[13]www.ft.com/content/56dde36c-aa40-11e9-984c-fac8325aaa04

Simulation

While data is growing at a dramatic pace, there is a nagging issue: a lot of the data is not useful or good quality. This is particularly troubling for advanced AI use cases, such as with self-driving cars. Even if a company collects data from cars that drive millions of miles, there will be many important scenarios that are missed.

What to do then? Does this mean something like autonomous vehicles are impossible? Not necessarily, although this technology has certainly proven extremely challenging.

Data scientists are finding creative ways to deal with the data shortages. One approach is to use simulations.

"Sometimes data is difficult to acquire for the conditions you want the AI system to find," said Paul Pilotte, who is the AI technical marketing lead at MathWorks. "For example, you could have a hydraulic pump with failure conditions like a worn bearing or a seal leak that you want to find. These conditions rarely happen and are destructive, making it very difficult to get failure data to train an AI model. That's where simulation comes in. You can use a model of the pump and run simulations to produce signals representing failure behavior, signals that can be used to train an AI model to detect the future occurrence of it on real systems in the field. The combination of automated tools to label data and simulation to generate synthetic data are key tools to help teams create the labeled data needed for AI systems."[14]

A company that has been on the leading edge of simulation is Waymo, which is Google's self-driving unit. Researchers from Waymo have created SurfelGAN, which uses texture mapping to come up with richer scenes from camera data. While simulators are not necessarily new, this one is generally more versatile because it can create data with a myriad of distances and angles. The system also does this with fairly low needs for computations. This means that SurfelGAN can work in real time. And as the name implies, this AI uses a generative adversarial network (GAN), which is useful in data creation. SurfelGAN also does not need labeled data.[15]

How Much Data Do You Need?

In many cases, you will need a large amount of data for an AI project. There is Hughes Phenomenon, which indicates that the more features you add to the model, the higher the accuracy.

---

[14]This is from the author's interview with Paul Pilotte on May 21, 2020.
[15]https://venturebeat.com/2020/05/20/waymo-is-using-ai-to-simulate-autonomous-vehicle-camera-data/

"One of the major challenges in machine learning is the data efficiency problem," said Ryan Sinnet, who is the CTO and co-founder of Miso Robotics. "While machines can often learn to be more accurate than humans, it takes machines a lot more practice than humans. You may be able to learn to recognize a new exotic vegetable from a handful of pictures whereas a machine may require several thousand pictures."

But there are definitely exceptions. In fact, a model can have too much data, which will result in a degrading of the effectiveness. This is known as the curse of dimensionality.

Thus, it's a good idea to not have any preconceived notions about how much data is needed. The fact is that some models may actually need very little amounts of data. According to Andrew Ng, who is the CEO of Landing AI and the former head of Google Brain, some projects may require only a mere 100 data points.

Consider the new field of study emerging in AI known as small data. It means that a model can be effectively and efficiently trained on small data sets.

An example of this is Google Research's new model, called Entities as Experts (EAE). It includes an assortment of people, organizations, times, figures, and so on. As for the model, it has been shown to solve complex natural language challenges without the need to use entity-specific knowledge.

For example, EAE was used to analyze Wikipedia posts that had more than 17 million entity mentions. But the system only needed to keep about one million of them to provide effective results.[16]

Data Problems

In New Zealand in March of 2019, a shooter live-streamed on Facebook his horrific killings of 50 people in two mosques. The online connection was not cut off until 29 minutes after the attack started. This meant that there were millions of views.

How was this possible? Part of this was due to bad actors who attempted to foil the Facebook system. But the underlying AI technology was ineffectual as well, primarily because of issues with the data.

In a blog post, Facebook's VP of Product Management, Guy Rosen, described this as follows: "AI systems are based on 'training data,' which means you need many thousands of examples of content in order to train a system that can detect certain types of text, imagery, or video. This approach has worked very well for areas such as nudity, terrorist propaganda, and also graphic violence

---

[16]https://venturebeat.com/2020/04/20/googles-entities-as-experts-ai-answers-text-based-questions-with-less-data/

where there is a large number of examples we can use to train our systems. However, this particular video did not trigger our automatic detection systems. To achieve that, we will need to provide our systems with large volumes of data of this specific kind of content, something which is difficult as these events are thankfully rare. Another challenge is to automatically discern this content from visually similar, innocuous content, for example if thousands of videos from live-streamed video games are flagged by our systems, our reviewers could miss the important real-world videos where we could alert first responders to get help on the ground."[17]

The lack of useful data has been a major issue with AI projects. Yet researchers and data scientists are finding creative ways to deal with this. Actually, this is one of the most important areas in the AI field and we'll likely see more innovations in the years ahead.

More Data Concepts

The data field definitely has lots of jargon. And it would not be possible to cover everything! But to end this chapter, let's take a look at a few other terms that you will likely encounter:

- *Categorical data*: This is data that does not have a numerical meaning. Instead, it is based on text, like a description of a group or category (say race or gender). But you can assign numbers to each of the elements.

- *Data type*: This is the kind of data a variable represents. Some examples include Booleans (true/false values), strings, integers, and floats (a number that has a decimal point).

- *Feature*: This is a column of data.

- *Instance*: This is a row of data.

- *Metadata*: This is data that describes other data. An example is a video file, which has metadata like size, date of the upload, comments, topic, and so on. Note that this type of data can be extremely useful in an AI model.

- *Ordinal data*: This is a mix of numerical and categorical data. An example is a five-star rating system on an app like Yelp.

- *Transactional data*: This is data generated from actions on ERPs and other enterprise systems.

---

[17]https://newsroom.fb.com/news/2019/03/technical-update-on-new-zealand/

Conclusion

You can easily get bogged down with data. This is why you need to be practical. There is no such thing as a perfect data set because there will always be issues and challenges. But as seen in this chapter, there are many best practices and automation tools that can streamline the process, which can get to effective outcomes quicker.

In the next chapter, we will take a look at AI model building.

Key Takeaways

- Data is essential for success with AI. It's a key reason why data-rich companies like Netflix, Google, Facebook, and Microsoft have been so successful with this technology.

- Data is growing at a rapid pace. According to IDC, the amount forecasted for the next three years will be the equivalent of what has been created for the past three decades. The COVID-19 pandemic is a major catalyst for growth, as there has been an accelerated shift to data-intensive technologies like videoconferencing.

- There are four main types of data: structured data, unstructured data, semi-structured data, and time-series data.

    - *Structured data*: This is information stored in spreadsheets and databases. For the most part, this type of information is fairly easy to use in AI models. However, there is generally less structured data available to work with.

    - *Unstructured data*: Examples include images, emails, videos, text files, satellite images, and social media messages. The majority of data is unstructured.

    - *Semi-structured data*: This is a blend of structured and unstructured data.

    - *Time-series data*: This shows interactions of data, such as with the "customer journey." The data can be structured or unstructured.

- Big data has three key attributes: volume, variety, and velocity, which are known as the three Vs.

  - *Volume*: This describes the huge scale of the data, at least in the tens of terabytes.

  - *Variety*: This shows the diversity of data, say with structured, unstructured, and semi-structured sources.

  - *Velocity*: This focuses on the speed that the data is generated. This is perhaps the most challenging part of big data.

- Over the years, other Vs have emerged: visualization of the data, value (how effective the information is), veracity (whether the sources can be trusted), and so on.

- A relational database has several features that make it much easier to work with data. At the heart of this technology is SQL or Structured Query Language, which is an English-like scripting system that helps to create tables, read them, make updates, and handle deletions. But relational databases also allow for making relationships among the tables.

- Yet relational databases certainly have their downsides, such as data sprawl and difficulties handling modern-day use cases like unstructured data and high-velocity data.

- Over the years, there have emerged next-generation databases to deal with the problems. One technology is the data warehouse, which efficiently handles large amounts of data. But there has also been the development of NoSQL databases. They use a document model, which provides a high degree of flexibility.

- The data lake has also become important. This makes it possible to have massive storage of data of any format.

- Then there is the feature store. This is a next-generation database that is built specifically for AI and ML.

- When it comes to developing AI projects, the data preparation is usually the most time-consuming. Despite this, many companies still do not devote enough resources to this part of the process. Yet problems with data are often the main reason why an AI project fails.

- Data collection is the first step in the data preparation process. You need to get an inventory of the assets of the organization. Then, you can look elsewhere for data sources, which may involve paying for licenses to third-party databases. But there are also many freely available sources, such as from the government.

- The next step is to evaluate the data. This involves seeing if the data is relevant, timely, and representative of the population. There should also be a legal review to see if the data can be used and if the IT infrastructure is able to handle the storage and processing.

- Data wrangling is a critical step. It is about improving the quality of the data set, such as dealing with missing items, duplications, and so on. There are automation tools that can help with this process. But someone with data science expertise needs to provide assistance.

- Labeling data is tedious and time consuming. Now there are automation tools to help out but they usually have limitations. Because of this, many companies will still use people for labeling. There are a variety of companies that provide this service, such as by using crowdsourcing.

- While many AI applications need enormous amounts data, there are still use cases where the needs are far less. Even a dataset of only 100 items can be enough.

Creating the Model

Where the AI magic happens

The Rubik's Cube, which is the 3-D puzzle that stirred up a craze during the 1980s, continues to challenge many people. But data scientists at OpenAI saw it as an interesting game to learn more about AI. In October 2019, the company announced it created a model that used a robotic hand to solve the Rubik's Cube. You can find the video on YouTube (https://bit.ly/3f5fuy4).

What's interesting about this is that the robotic hand was not cutting-edge. It had been developed 15 years earlier. Rather, OpenAI wanted to show how powerful algorithms can transform physical systems.

The company's researchers used deep learning, reinforcement learning, and Kociemba's algorithm. They used simulations for training, which got more and more complicated. For the most part, this is how the AI system was able to learn to solve the Rubik's Cube. This involved not only understanding the enormous number of combinations— 43,252,003,274,489,856,000 combinations, or 43 quintillion—but also the use of computer vision and coordination with the robotic hand. According to the OpenAI blog: "We focus on the problems that are currently difficult for machines to master: perception and dexterous manipulation."[1]

---

[1] https://openai.com/blog/solving-rubiks-cube/

© Tom Taulli 2021

T. Taulli, *Implementing AI Systems*, https://doi.org/10.1007/978-1-4842-6385-3_6

The end result: The AI was able to solve the Rubik's Cube about 60% of the time, depending on the environment. No doubt, OpenAI will continue to push the innovation to improve the accuracy rate.

This example illustrates how amazing AI can be. But it also shows the inherent power of algorithms. They can definitely be transformative.

True, for most organizations, there isn't the luxury of this kind of experimentation. But AI models do hold the potential for making notable improvements and can certainly be a key driver for business performance.

So in this chapter, we'll take a look at how to create solid AI models.

Model Selection

When it comes to model selection, it's a good idea to be creative and experiment with a variety of algorithms (keep in mind that there are hundreds available). This process has become much easier because of the availability of open source and proprietary AI platforms (we will cover some of them later in this chapter).

Yet there is a temptation to just focus on the accuracy. But this can lead to outcomes that are far from ideal. How so? For example, suppose that Model A has an accuracy rate of 85% and Model B is at 80%. However, Model A takes 10 times more time to train and is much more expensive. So is the extra 5% really that important? For many business applications, the answer may actually be "not very."

There are other issues to take under consideration when evaluating a model:

- How much data does it need? Does your organization have the right kind? Is there enough quality data?

- Can the model be explained? This is very important. When rolling out AI in a company, there can be much resistance. But if the model makes inherent sense to those who are non-technical, then adoption may be easier.

- How hard is it to maintain and deploy the model?

- Is there a need for a third-party audit?

It's a good idea to first test out simple models. You may realize that there is no need for something like a neural network or deep learning. Instead, the results from, say a regression model, may be good enough for your project.

Also, by starting with simpler models, you can establish baselines. This will help provide structure for the evaluation process.

Now even though software systems can help with the model selection process, the expertise of an experienced data scientist can go a long way. Such a person can often find a set of models that meet your requirements.

"As soon as the problem becomes more complicated because of a more complex task, messier data, or more innovative required solutions, then classic prepackaged or automated applications might not be enough any longer," said Rosaria Silipo, who is a PhD and a Principal Data Scientist at KNIME. "Some more creative and innovative thinking may be necessary, and your experience with past projects could be the key to the final solution. So data science is still kind of an art, where experience and knowledge play a determining role to find the optimal, and sometimes the only, possible solution."[2]

But of course, when selecting a model, there needs to be a focus on the problem to be solved. Here are some examples:

- If you are looking at categorical questions, such as "Is this a risky customer?" then you might want to look at algorithms for classification and perhaps clustering.

- If you are making a prediction for a numeric value, say for the value of a home, then a regression model might be a good option.

- If you have a set of time-series data for the customer journey, then you could employ a long short term memory (LSTM) network or a recurrent neural network (RNN).

- If you are working on a computer vision application, then you would look at RNNs and convolutional neural networks (CNNs).

- If you are developing a natural language processing (NLP) application, then you would consider bag of words, the Naive Bayes algorithm, topic modeling, and LSTM.

So what about creating unique AI models? This is definitely something that can be incredibly powerful. Some companies will even seek patents on their models. But it's important to note that you will likely need PhDs on your staff who have a deep understanding of AI. This is not practicable for most companies. But the good news is that publicly available models should be more than sufficient for most projects.

---

[2]From the author's interview with Rosaria Silipo on June 12, 2020.

Despite the different approaches, it's important to note that there is no right or wrong model. Rather, it's about finding a model that is appropriate for your business goals and the underlying data. Actually, it's common that several models work just fine.

But consider that in model building there is a well-known concept called the No Free Lunch Theorem, which means that no model is best for all tasks. There will always be some inherent limitations.

Ensemble Models

With the model selection process, there may be occasions when there should be more than one used. This is known as an ensemble model.

This does add to the complexity. But if an ensemble model is done properly, the results can be robust.

An example of this is Netflix. Back in 2006, the company established the Netflix Prize, which offered $1 million for any person or team that could improve the accuracy of the recommendation engine by at least 10%. To this end, the company open sourced a data set that had more than 100 million ratings of 17,770 movies from 480,189 users. It was a gold mine for ambitious data scientists!

At the time, Netflix was actually having challenges with its own models. It was essentially reaching diminishing returns. So why not try crowdsourcing?

The contest did inspire many people to participate, and there were lots creative solutions. Yet the goal proved to be a challenge.

However, a few years later, a team called BellKor's Pragmatic Chaos won the contest. To do this, they created a baseline model that helped to mitigate some of the problems with the data. After all, some movies had sparse ratings while others had large numbers. There were also some users who would always give low ratings and others who would just provide top ones! Like any data set, it was messy and required considerable normalization.

But there was another hurdle: the model testing. All in all, the team faced some tough issues. For example, an algorithm may continue to recommend the same films, there may not be the right genre for a particular firm, or there could be changes in the ratings over time (as societal tastes or attitudes evolve).

To deal with all this, the team used ensemble modeling. In fact, this meant using hundreds of algorithms. But in the end, the approach worked extremely well.

Training the Model

After you have identified the different algorithms for the project, you will then want to train them. Basically, can they learn and provide sufficient predictions?

You do this by using a data set. The first step is to randomize the information. By doing this, there will be less likelihood that the model will detect false patterns. Next, you need to divide the data sets into different sections, which will help to provide more accurate outcomes.

So let's take a look at the process.

Phase 1: Testing

This will involve anywhere from 70% to 80% of the data set. As you apply this data to the different models, there will often be varying results. Some will be fairly useless. But when it comes to modeling, there needs to be considerable trial and error.

In this phase, you will have to engage in some fine tuning of the model, such as with the parameters (each new iteration is called a "training step"). We'll look at the process later in this chapter.

Phase 2: Validation

This is where you have a sample of 10% to 20% of the data set. Given that the models have been tweaked, there should be an improvement in the accuracy. But in this stage, there should be analysis to see if there are problems like

- *Overfitting*: This is where the model is essentially memorizing patterns and has not effectively learned from the data. One of the signs of this is if there is a very high accuracy rate, say over 90%. So how can the overfitting be reduced? One approach is to collect more diverse data, which should help provide for a more robust model. What's more, using a less complicated algorithm could help with the overfitting.

- *Gaps*: The validation may show that the model has difficulties recognizing certain elements. For example, if you have an NLP app, one potential problem is that the AI will not be able to detect various words. If this is the case, then you probably need to add new features.

- *Underfitting*: This is where the model does not adequately reflect reality. Some ways to deal with this include increasing the number of parameters or use a more advanced algorithm.

Phase 3: Holdout Set

This is also called the "testing data." It includes 5% to 10% of the data set. Regardless of the name, this phase will give a final assessment of the overall accuracy of the model. The goal is to get a sense of how the AI reacts in a real-world environment.

Cloud-Based Model Systems

The training of an AI model does involve complex coding, such as with Python. While we will not show how this is done in this book, since the focus is for readers who are non-technical, there are still simple ways to build models.

Take a look at Teachable Machine from Google (`https://teachablemachine.withgoogle.com/`). By using drag-and-drop and pull-down menus, you can create your own AI model. First, you gather the data, such as from your photos. You can even upload audio files. Then you train the model. Note that Teachable Machine provides a myriad of options to tune the parameters to get better results. Finally, you can export the model and even host it on the Internet for free. Figure 6-1 shows what the app looks like.

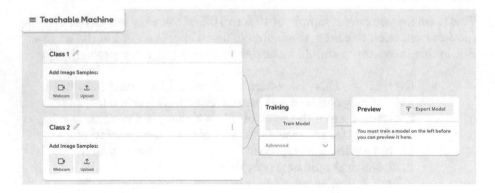

Figure 6-1. This is the interactive model creation system called Teachable Machine

Another interesting AI tool is the Machine Learning Playground (`https://ml-playground.com/`). Similar to the Teachable Machine, the workflow is easy. But the Machine Learning Playground provides a myriad of different models to apply to your data sets like k-nearest neighbors, support vector machines, artificial neural networks, and so on. Figure 6-2 shows what this looks like.

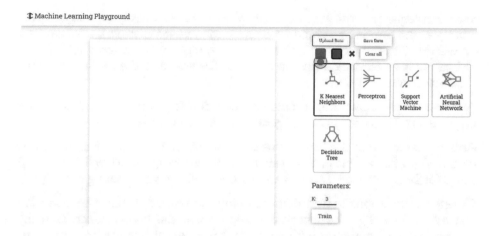

Figure 6-2. *The Machine Learning Playground is an AI model creation system*

Feature Engineering

After you have identified one or more models for the AI project, it's time for feature engineering. Keep in mind that this is the most important part of the model development process. Even a few wrong moves can mean that the results will be subpar.

To make any model work, you need to find those values that help predict results or learn new patterns. These values are the features.

Let's take an example. Suppose you want to predict the weather and you have a large data set for this. What are the features? Some data to consider would be the temperature, barometric readings, and perhaps radar information.

As you can see, this process involves some understanding of the domain. Thus, when it comes to feature engineering, an approach is to have experts help out (in this example, this would probably be a meteorologist). They should be able to quickly come up with the kinds of metrics and variables that are material. This process is called hand-crafting features.

But this does not mean feature engineering should only be for experts. Having a brainstorming session with the team can also be a good idea. Hey, even experts can be too narrow and miss important patterns.

In certain cases, the data will be non-mathematical. This means you will need to do a conversion. An example is if you are creating a model to determine if a tumor is malignant or benign. You may identify features such as tumor size and tumor shape.

Seems straightforward? Not necessarily. Features can easily be fuzzy. In this example, the tumor size could be expressed in terms of radius, surface area, or weight. Oh, and for shape, there are even more ways to look at this. You ultimately have to decide on the types of features and then have a number that represents them.

As this example shows, the complexity can increase greatly when using feature engineering. The process also is generally time-consuming.

Another issue is that the features usually are not transferable. What does this mean? With this example, the measurements for lung tumors will not be the same for breast cancer. This can add to the challenges of creating models.

Consider that sophisticated deep learning models can actually be used for feature engineering. The algorithms will crunch the numbers across many hidden layers to come up with patterns, often which humans are unable to detect. However, using deep learning may still not be enough. Having a human in the loop is usually advisable for feature engineering.

Deep learning models can also lead to terrible results. Sometimes they may be downright comical! Take the following real-world example from Sheldon Fernandez, who is the CEO of DarwinAI: "One of our automotive clients encountered some bizarre behavior in which a self-driving car would turn left with increasing regularity when the sky was a certain shade of purple. After months of painful debugging, they determined the training for certain turning scenarios had been conducted in the Nevada desert when the sky was a particular hue. Unbeknownst to its human designers, the neural network had established a correlation between its turning behavior and the celestial tint."[3]

■ **Note**   In feature engineering, you often will have two variables that are highly correlated. The best practice is to either drop one or combine the two so as to avoid inaccurate outcomes.

Parameters vs. Hyperparameters

The words "parameters" and "hyperparameters" are often used interchangeably. But this is a mistake. They each have important distinctions with AI models. But as should be no surprise, the terms can be very confusing.

A parameter is a variable that is internal to the model and whose value is determined from the underlying data. Then what are some examples? One would be the weights for a deep learning model. These values are optimized using algorithms.

---

[3]From the author's interview with Sheldon Fernandez on December 11, 2018.

As for a hyperparameter, this is a value that is external to the model and cannot be estimated from the data. How so? The reason is that a data scientist will specify the hyperparameters (the process is called hyperparameter tuning), such as by using a heuristic (that is, a "rule of thumb"). For example, the k-nearest neighbor classification algorithm requires the use of hyperparameters because there is no approach to calculate the exact value.

There are many machine learning programs that can provide automated hyperparameter tuning. This involves indicating the variables you want to have variation on and setting a metric as what thresholds to achieve. The system will then optimize the hyperparameters, which often use search algorithms like Bayesian optimization, grid search, and random search.

Accuracy

In the summer of 2018, the ACLU published a blockbuster blog post. It showed that Amazon.com's facial recognition software, called Rekognition, had some glaring deficiencies. The ACLU ran the system against photos of the members of the U.S. Congress against a database of mugshots. The outcome? 28 were identified as having been arrested for crimes! The false results disproportionately favored minorities, including Congressman John Lewis. For the ACLU, it only had to shell out $12.33 to use the model.

According to the blog post: "An identification—whether accurate or not—could cost people their freedom or even their lives. People of color are already disproportionately harmed by police practices, and it's easy to see how Rekognition could exacerbate that. A recent incident in San Francisco provides a disturbing illustration of that risk. Police stopped a car, handcuffed an elderly Black woman, and forced her to kneel at gunpoint—all because an automatic license plate reader improperly identified her car as a stolen vehicle."[4]

It's really chilling—and shows how AI accuracy can be high stakes. It is also an important reminder that the technology still has a long way to go.

So when evaluating accuracy, there needs to be much thought on the consequences. True, there will be many cases where you do not need high levels, such as when calculating churn or conversation rates for sales.

On the other hand, there are some areas where accuracy is perhaps the most important metric. This is usually the case for areas like medicine, finance, autonomous vehicles, and so on. If you are diagnosing for cancer, the AI system better be right. Likewise, if a person goes to an ATM, an accuracy rate of 99% would be completely unacceptable.

---

[4]www.aclu.org/blog/privacy-technology/surveillance-technologies/amazons-face-recognition-falsely-matched-28

Earlier in this chapter, you looked at how to divide the data into different parts in order to train the model. Keep in mind that, in this process, there will be an evaluation of the accuracy rates. This will also be the case when engaging in feature engineering.

Algorithms will have their own usual accuracy measures. You saw this in Chapter 2. For example, with a regression analysis, you could use the standard error and R-squared. Or if you have a logistic regression, you can put together a confusion matrix.

For accuracy, you will also see the following terms: precision, recall and FI score. Let's take a look at each of them. First, let's set up a matrix, as seen in Figure 6-1.

Table 6-1. A Matrix to Illustrate Precision, Recall, and the FI Score

	Predicted	
Actual	Yes	No
Yes	True positive	False negative
No	False positive	True negative

In the above, a true positive and true negative are when an outcome is a correct prediction. And yes, the false positives and false negatives are those with the incorrect predictions.

These concepts can definitely get fuzzy. So then, let's get a fuller explanation. Suppose we have a model that will output Yes if a tumor is cancerous and No if the tumor is benign. Then we process an X-ray and it outputs Yes, and when we check the patient's vitals, the person does have cancer. This would be a true positive since the model predicted Yes and the actual value was Yes.

But suppose we try another X-ray and we get something different. That is, the model predicts that there is no cancer and the actual value is No.

Well, when it comes to this analysis, we want true positives and true negatives because they are accurate predictions. On the other hand, we want to avoid these:

- *False positives*: This is where the model indicates cancer but the patient actually does not have the disease.

- *False negatives*: With this, the model predicts no cancer but the person does have the disease.

Given our matrix then, we can compute various metrics. One is the simplest: accuracy. This shows the number of correct predictions divided by the total predictions or

(True positives + true negatives)/(True positives + true negatives + false negatives + true negatives)

However, the accuracy metric can be misleading if there is a disproportionate number of false positives or false negatives. This is why we have metrics like the following:

Precision

This is calculated as follows:

True positives/(True positives + false positives)

This essentially takes into the account the false positives. Thus, if the accuracy is fairly high, say over 60%, then there is a lower risk of false positives.

Recall

This is computed as the following:

True positive/(True positive + false negative)

Yes, this accounts for the false negatives. So if the accuracy is high, then there is less of a likelihood of false negatives.

F1 Score

This is the weighted average of the precision and recall computations. In other words, the F1 score metric is more comprehensive, giving an overall indication of the false positives and false negatives.

The use of precision, recall and the F1 score can be critical in certain use cases. This is especially the situation with medical analysis. For instance, if you are diagnosing a potentially life-threatening disease, then you may want to allow for having false negatives but no false positives. This is why this type of analysis will involve having an expert review for all the results. By combining AI with a physician's expert judgement, there are often better results.

While all these approaches are quite useful, sometimes it is important to get a sample of some of the incorrect predictions. Was the result downright egregious? Did the model mistake a lightbulb for a TV? If so, there could be serious flaws with the algorithms even though the accuracy rate may be high.

AI Tools

According to G2.com, there are nearly 100 platforms to help build AI models. So it is really impossible to check them all out. And there are also new ones popping up.[5]

Many of the tools are also open source. This means that the software is free to use, although some of the systems may have restrictions and premium versions.

Yet this does not mean you should avoid proprietary platforms. Consider that these solutions may be more intuitive and automated. They may also have stronger backing, such as from venture capitalists.

So in the next part of this chapter, we will look at both open source and proprietary platforms.

Open Source Tools

With open source AI platforms, you will usually work with a computer language. By far, the most popular is Python. It is the fastest growing programing language in the world.

The mastermind of Python is Guido van Rossum, who launched the system in late 1989. The timing was spot on. The Internet was starting to emerge, especially in the academic community. The language was also fairly easy to learn and worked seamlessly with statistics and machine learning.

■ **Note**   van Rossum named Python after his favorite comedy, ***Monty Python's Flying Circus***.

But there are other reasons for the huge success of Python. One is that it became a must-have for the global academic community. And there was strong adoption from businesses and startups.

The open source model has also been essential. This has meant that thousands of developers have contributed to the evolution of the language, such as with new features, packages, and add-ons.

---

[5]www.g2.com/categories/data-science-and-machine-learning-platforms

Some of the popular add-ons, especially for machine learning and AI, include

- *NumPy*: This is an advanced system that helps to develop extensive indexes, matrices, slicing, tensors, masking, and multi-dimensional arrays. NumPy is written in both Python and C, which has helped improve the speed and efficiency. Note that the system has been optimized to be used with GPUs.

- *Pandas*: This add-on is focused on data analysis and cleanup as well as visualizations. This system also uses the C language for better performance.

A common way to work with Python is to use a Jupyter Notebook. This is a web app that allows for coding in the language in a structured manner (the commands are entered in cells). The code and scripts can then be shared with other programmers or made publicly available.

Besides Python, there is the R language. Its origins go back to 1993, when Ross Ihaka and Robert Gentleman teamed up to create a platform that would work better with statistics and visualizations. R is widely used for AI and some of the customers include Google, Airbnb, Uber, and Facebook.

OK then, now let's take a look at some of the top open source AI platforms:

TensorFlow

As deep learning became an important part of AI, Google realized it needed to use this technology. Its massive data sets were ideal for this and there was a need to provide more automation for its huge platforms.

But there was a nagging issue: There were no effective tools to create the deep learning models.

So Google developed its own, which was called TensorFlow. The project started in 2011 as a part of the Google Brain division. TensorFlow worked quite well and proved critical for next-generation apps.

But Google did something else that was noteworthy. In 2015, the company made TensorFlow open source. Why give it away? A major reason for this was that Google wanted to accelerate the innovation of AI. And this certainly happened—and quickly. The result is that TensorFlow has turned into an industry standard.

Consider that you can program TensorFlow in R, Swift, and JavaScript. But Python is the most popular.

TensorFlow operates by creating a tensor structure, which is essentially a multidimensional array, and is able to process the flow of the data on a graph. Since it powers applications for Google (like the Photos app), TensorFlow is robust for the most intense environments, whether on the desktop, mobile, edge devices, or clusters.

PyTorch

Facebook is the developer of PyTorch, which was launched in early 2016. The initial focus was on applications for computer vision and NLP. Given the rapid evolution of the platform, PyTorch has become a worthy rival of TensorFlow.

PyTorch was built to allow quick iterations, which is important for the model creation process. This is why the platform has become quite popular for researchers. But the system is also user-friendly and leverages the resources of Python.

Keras

Keras is an AI platform that is geared primarily to beginners. With just a few lines of code, you can create a sophisticated neural network. Even experts can use Keras as it can be good for quick experiments and prototypes.

According the website: "Keras is an API designed for human beings, not machines. Keras follows best practices for reducing cognitive load: it offers consistent and simple APIs, it minimizes the number of user actions required for common use cases, and it provides clear and actionable error messages. It also has extensive documentation and developer guides."[6]

Despite the simplicity, Keras is still powerful. Consider that TensorFlow has integrated the technology in its own platform.

Scikit-Learn

This is a full-blown AI platform, providing for the development of supervised and unsupervised models. Like Keras, the interface is easy to use. Yet the technology is strong enough for deploying enterprise applications.

Scikit-Learn is one of the older AI platforms; the project was started in 2007. It was part of an initiative from David Cournapeau for the Google Summer Code program. By the following year, Matthieu Brucher took on Scikit-Learn for his thesis. Then in 2010 the platform was publicly released. Since then, there has been a release cycle of about every three months.[7]

---

[6]https://keras.io/
[7]https://scikit-learn.org/stable/about.html

Proprietary Tools

The market for proprietary AI tools is massive – and it is likely to grow for the long haul. To get a sense of this, look at DataRobot. In November 2020, the company announced a whopping $270 million investment, which was led by Altimeter Capital. The valuation was set at $2.7 billion.[8]

This deal was not a one-off either. There have been a myriad of mega rounds for AI tools companies.

So then, who are some of the leaders in the space? Of course, mega tech operators like Microsoft, Amazon, and Google have their own platforms, which are based on their cloud offerings. Here's a look:

- *Azure Machine Learning*: This is Microsoft's suite of AI products, which includes internal systems but also third-party applications like Databricks and Keras. They are not just for data scientists. Microsoft also has applications geared for citizen developers and business analysts.

- *Google AI Platform*: There is BigQuery ML for handling massive data sets and access to the TensorFlow platform. The system also has easy-to-use AI applications for those who are not data scientists. Another interesting part of Google's system is the use of Kubeflow, which greatly helps with the deployment of applications. Finally, there is a thriving community of developers and researchers, such as with the AI Hub and Kaggle.

- *Amazon SageMaker*: The company has a huge advantage with its AWS (Amazon Web Services) platform. Thousands of customers already use this system to host their applications. This makes it easier to add AI capabilities. As for SageMaker, it is a full-blown system. "At Freshworks, we use AWS Sagemaker for distributed model training and workflow orchestration," said STS Prasad, who is the Freshworks EVP of Engineering. "Sagemaker enables us to train thousands of machine learning models in parallel for different customers and verticals."[9]

So now let's take a look at some of the other proprietary systems:

DataRobot

---

[8]www.datarobot.com/news/press/datarobot-announces-206-million-series-e-funding-round/
[9]From the author's interview with STS Prasad on June 7, 2020.

The company is one of the leaders in the AutoML space, which uses drag-and-drop and low-code approaches. DataRobot also handles all the key steps of model development and deployment (the program includes ten steps). The system can be used in the cloud or for on-premise environments and is integrated with AWS, Microsoft Azure, and Google Cloud.

According to research from Forrester, DataRobot demonstrated an ROI (Return on Investment) of 514% over a three-year period and a payback of less than three months. Note that the building and optimization of models took an average of 2.5 weeks, versus 13.5 weeks using other approaches.[10]

SAS

SAS is one of the early players in analytics and machine learning platforms. The company was founded in 1976 at North Carolina State University because there was a need for the USDA to analyze complex agricultural data. But this research would lead to opportunities across many other industries.

In the 1980s, the company revamped the software so it could run on any hardware or operating system. This certainly helped spur the growth. In fact, this strategy continues to be a key to the company's success today.

In terms of the AI capabilities, there was a release of SAS Viya in 2016. This allowed for much easier model creation and used a cloud-native architecture.

"Viya embeds key capabilities like machine learning, deep learning, computer vision, natural language processing (with conversational AI), forecasting, and optimization within the software so users have a seamless experience leveraging analytics capabilities to gain actionable insights and meet business needs," said Gavin Day, who is the Senior Vice President of Technology at SAS. "Viya also automates the process of data cleansing, data transformations, feature engineering, algorithm matching, model training, and ongoing governance, making it easier for both business analysts and data scientists to use SAS software. Results from queries are explained through natural language processing so data analyses are communicated in plain, easy to understand business terms."[11]

Then in 2019 the company announced its plan to invest $1 billion in AI technologies for a three-year period. This would include new products but also education and expert services.

Currently, SAS has close to 14,000 employees and 83,000 customer sites across the world. The company counts 91 of the top 100 companies on the 2019 Fortune 500 list as clients.

---

[10]https://3gp10c1vpy442j63me73gy3s-wpengine.netdna-ssl.com/wp-content/uploads/2020/05/ROI_Infographic_v.4.0.pdf

[11]From the author's interview with Gavin Day on June 15, 2020.

MathWorks

As you learned in Chapter 3, MathWorks is one of the pioneers of the analytics and machine learning tool markets. The company has two main products, MATLAB and Simullink. However, in terms of AI, MATLAB is really the one that is important to cover.

No doubt, an advantage for MathWorks is broad experience. This means that MATLAB has become a solid offering. It has a global ecosystem of users and partners. The system is also available across many platforms like on the edge, on-premise, and the cloud. You can even convert the algorithms to C/C++, HDL, or CUDA to be embedded in a processor for FPGA/ASIC.

Alteryx

Among the AI platform providers, Alteryx is the only pure-play operator that is publicly traded. The company launched its IPO in March 2017, with the stock price at $14. Since then, the shares have soared to $178 and the market cap has reached $12 billion.

Then again, Alteryx has been growing at a rapid pace. In the first quarter of 2020, the revenues jumped by 43% to $108.8 million and the company added 356 customers, including 12 of the Global 2000. In all, there are over 6,400 customers across the globe.[12]

According to Alteryx CEO and co-founder Dean Stoecker: "Competing, let alone winning in this data-driven world requires global enterprises to either disrupt themselves or be disrupted by others. It requires reimagining themselves, wherein data is valued as an asset and analytics as a prowess. This is not achieved by leveraging incumbent technologies and existing processes that made them great in the first place. And it cannot, in our view, be achieved by advocating analytics to only the trained statisticians working on edge cases, even with the best AI and ML capabilities. It can only effectively be achieved by harnessing the networking effects of people, data, and technologies, which allow companies to build a culture of data science and analytics that drives value across all functional areas of the organization. We believe this is best achieved with a human-centered platform that is code-free and code-friendly that liberates thinking, enables creativity, and analytics to address hundreds of use cases in every organization."[13]

The focus of Alteryx is to make its technology accessible by anyone. The system comes with hundreds of easy-to-use modules to build AI applications and models. There is also a robust data system, which ingests data sets from any source.

---

[12]https://investor.alteryx.com/news-and-events/press-releases/press-release-details/2020/Alteryx-Announces-First-Quarter-2020-Financial-Results/default.aspx

[13]www.fool.com/earnings/call-transcripts/2020/02/13/alteryx-inc-ayx-q4-2019-earnings-call-transcript.aspx

The company has also been smart with its acquisitions. To this end, it purchased ClearStory Data (automation of unstructured data) and Feature Labs (automation for feature engineering).

Dataiku

In 2013, the founders of Dataiku launched the company because they saw that using data was a strategic imperative. But the problem was that the available tools were simply not good enough.[14]

Its vision was certainly on target and the growth was immediate. As of now, hundreds of customers use Dataiku's technology to help with churn, fraud, predictive maintenance, and supply chain optimization.

In late 2019, the company announced a Series C funding round for $101 million, led by ICONIQ Capital. Other investors included Alven Capital, Battery Ventures, Dawn Capital, and FirstMark Capital.[15]

The Dataiku platform is called the Data Science Studio (DSS). A critical focus of the system is on allowing for teamwork and collaboration. As you've seen in this chapter, the model creation process involves numerous people across an organization, all with differing skillsets.

One of the company's marquee customers is BGL BNP Paribas, a global banking institution. The company uses the Dataiku platform to manage its fraud detection efforts. This is an area that requires ongoing attention, as security threats are constantly evolving. There is also the need to comply with changing regulations.[16]

While the company had its own set of machine language algorithms, they were difficult to update. So the company installed DDS, which took about eight weeks. This was also done with the necessary governance requirements.

However, the use of DDS was not limited to fraud detection. The system led to other projects to create more value.

Databricks

As you learned in Chapter 5, Databricks started as a project at UC Berkeley in 2009 and has since gone on to become a top player in the AI platform business. At the core of this is a sophisticated data infrastructure for all the steps in the model creation process. The system is based on Apache Spark, which is popular with machine learning. But Databricks is a contributor to other open source projects like Koalas, Delata, and MLFlow. And one of the most recent projects is Delta Lake, which helps clean up existing data lakes.

---

[14]www.dataiku.com/stories/the-dataiku-story/
[15]https://pages.dataiku.com/101million-series-c
[16]www.dataiku.com/stories/bgl-bnp/

The Databricks platform is cloud-based and available on AWS and Azure. Here are some of the use cases for the technology:

- It improves efficiencies for oil and gas companies. The machine learning is able to better discover and extract energy sources and help minimize downtime.

- Large pharmaceutical companies use Databricks to accelerate the drug development process. Databricks also quickly added COVID-19 data sets to the platform.

- Retailers are using the system to allow for personalized shopping experiences, such as with improved recommendations, pricing, and promotions.

An advantage of Databricks is that it allows a data scientist to use their preferred AI frameworks and libraries to interact with the underlying data. Then the model can be moved into production with a click. With a common UI, there are better feedback loops and collaboration.

Growth has been particularly strong for the company. In 2019, revenues exceed $200 million, up from $100 million on a year-over-year basis.[17] Customers include Hotels.com, Shell, Expedia, Regeneron, and Comcast.

KNIME

The roots of KNIME go back to 2004 when a team from the University of Konstanz created a platform to make it easier to manage and process data. The leader was Michael Berthold, who had a background in Silicon Valley. When the KNIME system was launched in 2006, there was much demand from the pharma industry. But over the years, the company has been successful in expanding across a myriad of verticals.

Consider that the KNIME Analytics Platform is open source but the KNIME Server is a proprietary solution that provides enterprise-level features like automation and collaboration. This combination is quite powerful, supporting the complete data science journey.

The KNIME open source system has a modern UI, which allows the user to drag-and-drop items on a canvas. This is much more intuitive than the typical script-based approach and allows for higher productivity.

---

[17]www.cnbc.com/2020/06/16/databricks-prepared-for-recession-with-fund-raising-real-estate-cuts.html

Other functions of KNIME include

- *Integrated deployment*: This is a workflow system that helps to minimize errors when deploying models. There are also a range of deployment options from a web-based dashboard and REST API service.

- *Data*: KNIME works with the most common data systems, such as SQL, NoSQL, cloud-based platforms, and on-premise databases.

- *Data wrangling*: You can use a variety of approaches like joining, concatenation, filtering, aggregations, and normalization.

- *Guide automation*: The whole data cycle can be automated, such as with ingesting, preprocessing, dimensionality reduction, outlier detection, and so on.

- *Model monitoring*: This handles issues with data drift or data jumps, which can distort models that have been deployed.

In-House AI Systems

The innovation with open source and proprietary AI systems continues at a rapid pace. But they all have their drawbacks. Let's face it, the AI process is highly complex and nuanced, and this is why some companies build their own solution. True, it may be expensive and time-consuming. But as AI becomes more strategic, an in-house system could wind up being a strong asset.

An example of a company that has gone down this route is Freshworks. Founded in 2010, the company operates a cloud platform that helps with customer engagement.

In late 2019, Freshworks raised $150 million from Sequoia Capital, CapitalG (which is affiliated with Google), and Accel at a valuation of $3.5 billion. The company has more 40,000 paying customers like Cisco, Hugo Boss, and Honda.[18]

Even though Freshworks has its own in-house system, the company still uses a variety of third-party tools. "At Freshworks, we use AWS Sagemaker for distributed model training and workflow orchestration," said STS Prasad, who is the EVP of Engineering at the company. "Sagemaker enables us to train thousands of machine learning models in parallel for different customers and

---

[18]https://techcrunch.com/2019/11/13/freshworks-raises-150m-series-h-on-3-5b-valuation/

verticals. We also use Apache Spark, Hadoop, Sci-kit, and R libraries for the most common machine learning algorithms. For deep learning, we use Keras and PyTorch frameworks and pre-trained deep learning models such as BERT and ELMo for embedding text."

Then what about the in-house AI systems? The focus is primarily on configurability and productivity for data scientists. For the most part, the goal is to find ways to get models productized as quickly as possible.

And yes, Freshworks used this to create an AI system called Freddy AI, which its customers can use. "Freddy AI continuously learns from all customer interactions across marketing, sales, and support," said Prasad. "The Freddy chatbot enables businesses to acquire, engage, and support customers without the need for manual intervention. Freddy AI learns from ticket data in our customer engagement product, Freshdesk, to help automate repetitive tasks, provide self-service for routine questions, and allow for contactless resolution of service requests."

Freddy AI operates on top of the Freshworks master customer record, consolidating data across the Freshworks suite of products to give organizations a 360-degree view of their customers. There are also heavy investments in conversational AI like agent response suggestions and type-assist features (similar to Gmail's smart complete)

"Every business is different, and each customer requires a certain level of configurability in order to make AI/ML features work to meet their needs," said Prasad. "Because of this, every Freddy AI feature comes with a standard set of admin configuration options that can be used to tailor its features to suit the unique needs of an organization. Another lesson is that our customers aren't just looking for the newest or trending AI capabilities, they're looking for features and actionable insights that drive business transformation. AI/ML initiatives have to be ROI positive for continued adoption."

Correlation Vs. Causation

There are a variety of rules of thumb when creating models. In this chapter, you've taken a look at some of them, such as dividing the data set into different sections.

Now these rules of thumb may not always be correct. However, they can still be quite helpful and streamline the AI process.

But there is another very important rule of thumb to keep in mind, and you do not have to be a data scientist to use it: Correlation is not causation. There are actually some comical examples of this. Just look at Tylervigen.com, which collects faulty correlations. Here are a few examples:

- The number of people who drowned by falling into a pool correlates with films Nicolas Cage appeared in.

- Per capita cheese consumption correlates with the number of people who died by becoming tangled in their bedsheets.

- The divorce rate in Maine correlates with per capita consumption of margarine.

It's kind of crazy. To this end, there is a concept known as patternicity, which means we have a tendency to detect patterns in meaningless noise!

The fact is that finding causation is extremely difficult and time-consuming. It usually involves extensive studies. For example, in medical research, there is research that involves randomized samples and control groups to see if certain conditions lead to a particular disease. One of the most famous examples of this involved the studies on smoking and lung cancer during the 1960s.

Something else about when using AI models: There are oftentimes interesting relationships that seem counterintuitive and yet are still spot on. These types of insights can certainly be a big driver for a business. Here are some examples:[19]

- People who completed a loan form correctly and without spelling errors had better risk profiles. This was less so for those who used all lower case.

- According to data from Xerox and other large companies, those employees who used Chrome and Firefox performed better. Why so? The theory is that these employees were willing to experiment and try new things to help improve their productivity.

■ **Note**   What's the difference between machine learning and artificial intelligence? If it's written in Python, it's probably machine learning. If it's written in PowerPoint, it's probably AI. In other words, when it comes to AI, there remains quite a bit of hype!

---

[19]https://blogs.scientificamerican.com/guest-blog/9-bizarre-and-surprising-insights-from-data-science/

Ending a Project

The best practices explained in this chapter will go a long way to improving the odds of success of an AI project. But unfortunately, there will likely be cases where a project may not be viable. This may come after much investment and iterations.

Yet this should not be seen as a failure. It is just an inevitable part of the process. AI is generally based on massive data sets and probabilities. As a result, it's impossible to guarantee a good outcome.

But a failed project should have a postmortem. Take an honest look at why it did not work out and what lessons were learned. This will certainly be essential for the next project.

Conclusion

In this chapter, you looked look at the steps and best practices for creating models. This is a challenging process but also engaging. You may learn an insight that could move the needle for your business. On the other hand, a project may just wind up being a failure. But with the process, you will continue to build your AI muscles.

OK then, regarding the next chapter, we will cover the deployment of AI.

Key Takeaways

- Model selection should start with experimentation. There are hundreds of algorithms available.

- But before selecting a model, you need to look at the quality of the data set, the deployment options, maintenance requirements, and any legal issues.

- It's usually best to start with simple models.

- Custom AI models are certainly powerful. But they usually require PhDs to create. Publicly available models are often sufficient for many business applications.

- An ensemble model is when more than one AI model is combined. This can lead to improved accuracy scores, although there will be increased complexity.

- An initial step in the training of an AI model is to randomize the data. This will help reduce the incidence of false patterns.

- The next step is to divide the data set into at least two parts. One of the segments will be for testing (which will have 70% to 80% of the information), such as to find the parameters and features of the model. After this, there will be a validation data set. This will be used to get a sense of how the model works in the real world. There will also be a look at issues like gaps in the data, underfitting, and overfitting.

- Model building is complex and requires technical skills. But there are some web-based systems that allow just about anyone to develop their own models. Examples include Teachable Machine from Google and the Machine Learning Playground.

- Feature engineering is about identifying the variables that are the best predictors for a model. This often means having a good understanding of a domain. For example, an expert should be able to come up with the typical factors that help explain certain patterns and systems.

- Sophisticated deep learning can be used to find features that are often not detectible by people. But this approach is far from perfect. There should still be a human in the loop to check the results.

- A parameter is a variable that is internal to the model and whose value is determined from the underlying data.

- A hyperparameter is a value that is external to the model and cannot be estimated from the data. A data scientist will specify the hyperparameter, using some type of rule of thumb. This is known as hyperparameter tuning. There are machine learning systems that can also automate this.

- Accuracy is the measure of the correct predictions divided by the total predictions. But there are many other ways to get a sense of the accuracy of a model. Some of these include metrics like precision, recall and the F1 score. They account for the false positives and false negatives in the model.

- There are a large number of AI tools. Some are open source, which means they are freely available. And others are proprietary and require a license or subscription. Both solutions have pros and cons. It all depends on what you want to accomplish with your AI efforts.

- Python is the most popular programming language for AI. It is relatively easy to learn and there is an extensive ecosystem of third-party add-ons like NumPy and Pandas.

- In some cases, a company will build in-house AI tools. This option is expensive but can be worth the effort, so long as the focus is on strategic capabilities.

- A key principle in AI is that "correlation is not causation." If you want to find the real cause of something, you must perform in-depth studies and analysis.

- Failure is common with AI models, even when there is a solid process. This is ok. But it is important to do a postmortem to see what happened.

Deployment and Monitoring

It's showtime!

In the summer of 2019, Apple launched its credit card, which involved a partnership with Goldman Sachs. It was designed to emphasize simplicity, privacy, and security (the card did not have a number, CVV security code, expiration date, or signature line). There were also no fees, the interest rates were competitive, and there was a good rewards program.

What about AI? It was a big part of the Apple Card. It was not only useful to help customers understand their spending but also to optimize the credit limits.

Cool, right? Definitely. But unfortunately, the AI had some glaring issues. The algorithms actually were biased. When Apple made an offer for credit lines, there were generally smaller ones for women vs. men! When customers realized this, they went straight to Twitter and made their displeasure known. Even legendary computer entrepreneur Steve Wosniak spoke out. His wife got a smaller credit limit even though her credit rating was higher than his.

© Tom Taulli 2021

T. Taulli, *Implementing AI Systems*, https://doi.org/10.1007/978-1-4842-6385-3_7

Apple's support team was caught off guard and stumbled badly. When handling incoming calls and texts, the explanation was an unsatisfactory: "It's just the algorithm."[1]

Goldman Sachs then said that the algorithms were not biased because they did not use gender as a factor in the model. The firm also noted that it used a third party to test the Apple Card for bias.[2]

But none of this was enough for customers. The plain fact was that the Apple Card was skewed. If anything, it was a demonstration that avoiding the use of data like gender does not necessarily matter. Other types of data may correlate with this anyway (this is known as a data proxy). For example, if you use a person's job description, this could bias the data for a certain gender.

This case study highlights how difficult deployment can be when it comes to AI. It also shows that some of the top companies can easily get things very wrong.

So in this chapter, we'll take a deeper look at how to be successful with deployment in the AI process.

Types of AI Deployments

At a high level, there are two main ways to deploy AI. The first one is called an analytical model, which is similar to a BI (business intelligence) tool. This means that employees use the system to get reports, find trends, and get insights. Note that the analytical model is the most common.

Next, there is an operational model, and this is the far more complicated approach. This is where AI is embedded in a product, such as Uber. This requires access to real-time information and sophisticated systems to update the models. Before an operational model is launched, there needs to be lots of testing and quality assurance. Even a small glitch can be damaging to a company's brand (as seen with the Apple Card example).

By and large, for those organizations that are starting with AI, the best approach is to focus on analytical models.

---

[1]www.forbes.com/sites/tomtaulli/2019/11/11/apple-card--did-ai-run-amok/#6837a2802e8b
[2]www.wired.com/story/the-apple-card-didnt-see-genderand-thats-the-problem/

MLOps

The category that involves handling the deployment and monitoring of AI Is called MLOps (this is short for "machine learning operations"). It is similar to DevOps, which is where there is a combination of software development and operational functions.

To help with MLOps, you can use an AI platform (we covered a variety of them in the prior chapter). Such a system will have guardrails to prevent noncompliance issues, monitoring of performance, and functions to help with the handing off to different teams. The result is that the process is streamlined and less prone to error. There is also more time for the data scientists to focus on building better models and other value-added activities.

As these AI platforms get more sophisticated, they are handling more of the workload and providing much-needed automation. But MLOps still requires putting together organizational structures and workflows for the teams. There must be coordination across many different types of functions like version control, testing, analytics/tracking, continuous integration, model score validation, debugging, configuration, data management, and so on. Putting this all together does take time and a commitment from management. If not, then even a successful AI model could fail because it will not be deployed properly.

For example, suppose it takes a couple months to deploy a model. Well, during this period of time, the accuracy may decay as the data goes stale. This is actually a very common problem with AI deployment.

Keep in mind that MLOps is still in the early stages and there is no standard approach. Because of this, Cloudera has announced its Cloudera Machine Learning (CML) MLOps organization, which involves numerous partners to develop open standards and best practices for governance.

Another key element for MLOps is the need to have an assessment of the current IT environment. What legacy systems are in place? Do some of them need to be replaced or modified? This is absolutely critical because there needs to be a solid foundation for AI deployment.

Testing

Quality assurance or the testing of an AI model is part of the role of the data scientist. As seen in the last chapter, they evaluate the results by looking at accuracy, precision, recall, and so on.

Yet a data scientist can easily miss issues. The fact is that AI is fairly open ended, which can make it challenging to think through the many possibilities.

This is why it's a good idea to have a QA person to focus solely on testing. Such a person may spot subtle problems but may also help with suggestions on the UI. Having an engaging user experience will go a long way in getting adoption across an organization or with customers.

An approach to consider for this is test-driven development or TDD. With it, you design tests for the functions of an AI application and, interestingly enough, you want them to fail (Figure 7-1 shows the process). In other words, you want to think in terms of cracking the system. The next step is to create code that makes sure that the test will pass. After this, there is often some refactoring or improvements to the code.

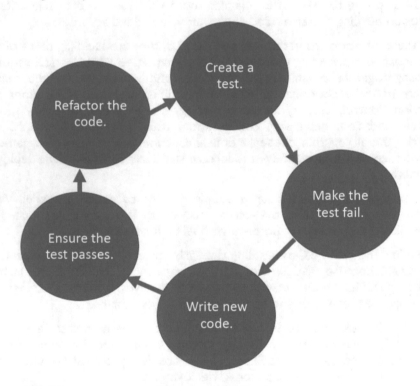

Figure 7-1. This shows the process for test-driven development

Sounds kind of tedious? It is. But the TDD approach really does lead to higher quality code. There is also much more emphasis on it being modular, and this makes it easier for modifications.

There are certainly a myriad of tools that can help with the testing process. They can provide assistance with areas like data analysis systems to detect problems like bias and outliers and with debugging tools to find overfitting and underfitting

The UI

In 1996, Microsoft introduced Clippy as part of its Office platform. Clippy was an AI assistant that was in the form of a cartoon character (it was a paper clip with eyes!). But unfortunately, the user response was brutal.

This was despite the fact Microsoft had spent six months working on in-depth research. The company's designers actually came up with over 250 potential characters. Yet Clippy turned out to be the one that was most trustworthy and engaging, according to surveys.

But it didn't matter. When Clippy was deployed at scale, the results were downright awful.

This case certainly holds some valuable lessons for AI deployment. And yes, this means that UI really needs to be a priority.

So then, what are some of the takeaways with Clippy? How is it possible to avoid the problems?

Let's take a look:

- *Little things matter*: A big problem with Clippy was its eyes. Some people thought they were … creepy.

- *Diversity*: The team that created Clippy was predominantly male and white. This likely influenced the characteristics and gestures of the figure. Consider that many women saw Clippy as off-putting.

- *First use*: Clippy would pop up when it looked like you were writing a letter (such as when you started with "Dear"). This was helpful. But when Clippy kept showing up for the same things, the experience became annoying.

- *Capabilities*: When Clippy was released, PCs were still constrained in terms of memory and capabilities. This meant that the AI was basic and this was a key reason why failure was common. For the most part, Microsoft was setting up unrealistic expectations.

Coming up with compelling UIs is tough and takes experimentation. But it is well worth the effort.

"The results of the data science project will be offered to the final users, usually non-data science experts," said Rosaria Silipo, who is the principal data scientist at KNIME. "How much should the application GUI hide the complexity, and how much should be visible for customization by the end user? How important is the final GUI to allow the data science application to communicate with the end user? Well, the application GUI must be informative and yet at the same time easy to use. Just a few clicks to move across the application but plenty of interactivity when exploring the results."[3]

Monitoring

After an AI app has been launched—that is, put into production—there needs to be a focus on the operationalization. This means that the technology must be monitored and tracked to ensure the results are meeting your KPIs (key performance indicators).

After all, AI is evolving as it takes in new data. The goal is that it will get smarter and more effective over time. But then again, the reverse can happen as well. This is because the underlying circumstances of the model may change. This could lead to deteriorating results. This is known as model drift.

Let's take an example of this. When the COVID-19 pandemic hit, various AI models simply could not handle the impact. Keep in mind that they were based on a history of data that did not include sudden spikes in demand for toilet paper, hand sanitizer, paper towels, and N95 masks. Such items generally see fairly stable patterns. The bottom line: There was extensive disruption in supply chains, which took time to fix.

But the COVID-19 pandemic had other adverse consequences. One was for mapping. Since traffic fell to unprecedented levels, the AI systems were unable to effectively optimize the routes.

True, these are extreme examples. Yet they do highlight the fact that models make various assumptions, which often change.

AI tools can help deal with such things, such as by providing alerts. But there should be ongoing testing of the models in terms of the accuracy rates. If there is slippage, then the model probably needs to be updated.

Having people in the loop is definitely crucial for this. Take a look at Phrasee, which develops AI software to automate the creation of copy for email campaigns and other marketing efforts. When the COVID-19 pandemic hit, the company had to act swiftly to change its models. To this end, the data scientists avoided the use of phrases like "going viral," which would only alienate users. This even included avoiding the use of certain emojis that provoked fear.[4]

---

[3]From the author's interview with Rosaria Silipo on June 12, 2020.
[4]www.technologyreview.com/2020/05/11/1001563/covid-pandemic-broken-ai-machine-learning-amazon-retail-fraud-humans-in-the-loop/

Note   Here's another AI joke. An AI walks into a bar and the bartender asks, "What are you having?" The AI says, "What did the last 10,000 people have?"

Security

Besides the need for monitoring of the models, there must also be an emphasis on security. AI models often include sensitive data. Any breach could result in substantial fines and reputational damage. Thus, when creating an AI application, there needs to be an ongoing evaluation of security measures. This means reaching out to IT and the legal department to make sure the organization's policies are in place.

Consider that AI is increasingly being used to pull off cyberattacks. The first known case of this came in 2007, with the CyberLover chatbot. It used NLP (natural language processing) to provide personalized responses to users that resulted in higher conversions of links to steal personal information.[5]

In some cases, the impact has been on a wide scale. Take the example of TaskRabbit, an online marketplace for freelancers. In 2018, it suffered an attack that impacted 3.75 million user accounts, which resulted in the exposure of Social Security numbers and bank account information.[6]

There has also emerged something called AML or adversarial machine learning. This is where someone creates malware with the intention of destabilizing an AI model (it's also known as "model poisoning"). This usually involves flooding the system with new data, such as false positives, that distorts the training set. For the most part, such an attack can be difficult to detect.

Another vulnerability is with sensors, like with IoT (Internet of Things) systems. They can be hijacked and the data manipulated.

No doubt, the risks are scary and they are getting more sophisticated. This is why it is important to have a solid security strategy. It is usually a good idea to bring in a consultant who can secure the data and models.

Return on Investment

While monitoring the AI app, there should be a periodic assessment of the ROI (return on investment). And yes, there are various approaches to calculating this, although, given that AI provides long-term benefits, there probably should be some latitude. The early investments will likely be

---

[5]www.darkreading.com/vulnerabilities---threats/malicious-use-of-ai-poses-a-real-cybersecurity-threat/a/d-id/1337690
[6]www.infoq.com/articles/ai-cyber-attacks/

significant and there will be failed projects, which will depress the ROI in the early stages. This is why senior management needs to take a long-term view with AI. It is about a strategic opportunity that can potentially transform a business.

OK then, so when looking at ROI, let's first see the cost side of the equation. Some of the components include

- Computer power and storage
- Consulting fees, such as for the creation of the model, UI design, and integration with the existing IT infrastructure. There may also be a need to hire a subject matter expert (SME).
- Data acquisition
- Training the users of the AI application
- Costs for maintenance and support
- Compensation for data scientists, data engineers, AI solution architects, AI testers, and machine learning engineers
- Licenses or subscriptions for AI software platforms

AI also has unique aspects that make it different from a typical software project when it comes to the costs. How so? Well, consider an analysis from venture capitalists at Andreessen Horowitz that has the following interesting insights:

- Training an AI model can be expensive in terms of computer power. The potential costs could be in the six figures. But these are usually not one-time costs since data and models change over time.
- Model inference, which is about coming up with predictions while the AI app is in production, is much more complex than traditional software. The reason is the series of matrix multiplications.
- Storage costs can be significant since many AI applications use images, video, and audio.
- Even with the various AI tools, the data preparation process is still a highly manual process.
- AI applications can be challenging to scale in the cloud because of latency issues. As a result, a company may need to have trained models spread across different regions.

According to the post: "Taken together, these forces contribute to the 25% or more of revenue that AI companies often spend on cloud resources. In extreme cases, startups tackling particularly complex tasks have actually found manual data processing cheaper than executing a trained model."[7]

This is not an argument against AI. Andreessen Horowitz remains a major investor in the space and is quite bullish on the prospects. However, an AI project does need a conservative approach with the budget and it may take some time to get efficiencies.

Note that there is another cost that is often overlooked: the cost of doing nothing. In other words, this could mean being put at a competitive disadvantage to competitors, which could lead to lower growth or even extinction.

So now, let's take a look at the "return" part of the ROI calculation. The most common metric is to look at time saved. This could allow for employees to spend more time on value-add activities.

The calculation for this is straightforward. Example: Suppose you are using AI to automate the processing of invoices. In your finance department, employees spend 200 hours a week on this activity. Assuming the average pay is $20 per hour, then the annual savings would come to $192,000. If the cost of the deployment of the AI system is $130,000, then the ROI would be 48%.

But there are intangible benefits for an AI project. It could be, for example, an improvement in the user experience of a mobile app or an increase in the NPS (Net Promoter Score), which is an effective measure of customer loyalty. For various industries, AI can even be used to help improve the safety of employees, such as with offshore oil rigs or mines.

In some cases, there may even be revenue opportunities. To this end, an AI system could use a recommendation system to cross-sell existing customers or there could be an optimization of the pricing. In fact, the ROI will often include several metrics.

Change Management

Change management involves the preparation and support of an organization to adopt something new. No doubt, AI needs this for success. But change management is particularly challenging and is a big reason for the failure of any new technology implementation.

---

[7]https://a16z.com/2020/02/16/the-new-business-of-ai-and-how-its-different-from-traditional-software/

AI may even more troublesome. Let's face it, there is often much fear from employees that they will lose their jobs or be transitioned to another role, which may have fewer opportunities. There are also the problems with handling legacy systems.

There are a variety strategies and frameworks for change management. But there is one that has proven to be quite effective and it is John Kotter's eight-step process. He came up with it during the mid-1990s (and it's the basis of his best-selling book, *Leading Change*). It's based on research on over 100 companies like GM, British Airways, and Bristol-Myers Squibb.

Here's a brief overview of his approach:

- *Create a sense of urgency*: This needs to come from senior management. It is about crafting a vision about the importance of the initiative. An example of this is what Mark Zuckerberg did in 2012. At the time, Facebook was lagging in its mobile phone efforts. But Zuckerberg took swift action and led by example. He greatly increased the usage of his own phone and even wrote the company's annual shareholder report with it.

- *Build a guiding coalition*: The senior management team is not the only influential group within an organization. There are always other people who have tremendous respect and authority. Thus, it is important to get their buy-in for the vision.

- *Form a change vision*: The vision needs a clear-cut destination that must be realistic, flexible, and attainable. This should be communicated in a brief manner, say in five minutes or less.

- *Communicate the vision*: Leaders in the organization must constantly talk about the vision. The fact is that it takes time for employees to internalize a new message.

- *Empower broad-based action*: Make sure that people are acknowledged for their efforts. And this should happen even if an initiative did not live up to expectations or even failed. The idea is that experimentation should be encouraged.

- *Generate short-term wins*: This helps to gin up momentum and enthusiasm. If not, there will likely be resistance to the vision.

- *Consolidate gains and produce more change*: There should not be the perception that the celebration of a quick win is the end of the journey. Change management needs to strike a balance between the short run and the long run.

- *Anchor new approaches in the culture*: Sustaining the change is challenging. It might be the toughest part of the process. This is why the leaders in the organization need to have constant communication of the vision.

With these principles, it is certainly possible to create an AI-driven organization. The idea is that there will be a focus on analyzing data, not just having hunches about certain things.

A company that has been a leader in this is Stitch Fix. Here's how the platform works: a user takes a survey to explain their fashion interests (the average client provides 90 data points) and then an AI system makes personalized clothing choices. As time goes by, Stitch Fix collects more data, which means that the results get better and better.

The company has 200 software engineers and 125 data scientists. According to its 10-K filing: "We use data science throughout our business, including to style our clients, predict purchase behavior, forecast demand, optimize inventory, and design new apparel."[8]

As a sign of the company's strategic focus on AI, it has a Chief Algorithms Officer, who is Eric Colson. Prior to joining Stitch Fix, he was the VP of Data Science and Engineering at Netflix.

In an article for the Harvard Business Review, Colson set forth some of his key principles for creating an AI-driven culture.[9] They include the following:

- Data science must be its own entity, not a subset of another department like product development or marketing. It should have a direct report to the CEO. Granted, the data science team will need to collaborate with other departments but this should be done on an equal basis.

- Data scientists need the resources required for success. This includes access to data, the ability to make hiring decisions, the authority to purchase sophisticated AI platforms, and the necessary computing systems. If there is an onerous budget process, this will stunt innovation.

---

[8]www.sec.gov/ix?doc=/Archives/edgar/data/1576942/000157694219000013/
stitchfix10kfy2019.htm
[9]https://hbr.org/2018/11/curiosity-driven-data-science

- Experimentation needs to be encouraged and rewarded. There also needs to be ongoing investment in training, not just for data scientists but the whole organization. Achieving data and AI literacy should be a strategic priority.

■ **Note**   In a study from Deloitte, of the 37% of the companies in the survey that exhibited strong analytics cultures, about 48% of them greatly exceeded their business goals for the past year.[10]

Deployment Case Study: Lemonade

In 2015, Daniel Schreiber and Shai Wininger launched Lemonade. The goal was to disrupt the traditional insurance industry by leveraging the power of AI. Both founders had strong backgrounds in the tech world. Schreiber was the former CEO of Powermat Technologies (a wireless charging company) and he started an Internet company during the late 1990s. Wininger was also a serial entrepreneur; his biggest venture was Fiverr International (NYSE:FVRR), an online marketplace for freelancers. The company has a market value of over $2 billion.

Consider that the insurance industry is perhaps the first industry that used data. It was during the 1600s that John Graunt created modern statistics and used probabilities to determine life expectancies. All this would result in one of the largest companies in England: Lloyd's of London.

Despite this, the insurance industry has generally lagged with cutting-edge technologies. But the founders of Lemonade saw this as a great opportunity. They built an extensive AI platform that includes the following:

- *AI Maya*: This is a bot that uses NLP to handle the collection of information, the creation of quotes, and the facilitation of payments. This has shown to greatly reduce onboarding times for new customers.

- *AI Jim*: This is the bot that manages insurance claims. AI Jim can handle the entire process and has been able to resolve matters in a third of the cases. And for those claims that cannot be processed by the bot, they are sent to the right person. Oh, and the resolution time is usually

---

[10]www2.deloitte.com/us/en/insights/topics/analytics/insight-driven-organization.html

quite low because AI Jim has done much of the heavy lifting. As should be no surprise, the claims process is the most delicate for an insurance company. So the fact that AI Jim is able to manage this effectively is a testament to the power of AI.

- *CX.AI*: This bot resolves customer requests and has been able to handle about a third of the cases. CX.AI can help with coverage questions, pre/post purchase inquires, changes to policies, and payments. By using this technology, Lemonade saw an 87% drop in the number of tickets processed by employees.

- *Forensic Graph*: This AI system uses behavioral economics and big data to predict, deter, and block fraud. Fraud accounts for $40 billion in waste for the insurance industry in the US.

- *Cooper*: This is an internal bot that runs various parts of the company. Just some of the processes it manages include processing paper checks and the running of thousands of tests for software releases. In fact, Cooper even analyzes the spectrometry imaging from NASA's satellites!

Of course, at the core of all this is a massive data repository. So Lemonade built the Customer Cortex to manage all this.

According to the company's SEC filing: "The power of our system goes beyond the sheer tonnage of data it generates, as we are able to put data to work in ways we believe, based on the experience of our management in the insurance industry, that legacy systems cannot. Our systems are entirely integrated, so data generated in a customer support interaction can inform the claims process, while claims data routinely impacts marketing campaigns, and so forth. Likewise, our bots do not merely collect data, but also adapt in real time in response to the data they collect."[11]

All in all, this is the cutting-edge of AI deployment and is likely to be a major competitive advantage, especially as Lemonade battles some of the world's largest companies.

---

[11]www.sec.gov/Archives/edgar/data/1691421/000104746920003943/a2242013z424b4. htm#cu40510_our_lemonade_stand_a_letter_from_our_co-founders

Conclusion

MLOps is something that will grow significantly in the years ahead. We will see new tools emerge and best practices evolve. The result will be much more powerful AI. Actually, as seen with companies like Lemonade, there can be the creation of breakout companies that transform industries.

In the next chapter, we'll take a look at responsible AI.

Key Takeaways

- There are two main types of AI deployment. First, there is the analytical model approach, which is similar to a BI tool. In other words, the AI generates reports to provide insights, say about customers. The analytical model is the most common.

- Then there is operational AI. This is where the AI is embedded in a product (an example is Uber). By far, this a much more complicated form of deployment and requires significant testing.

- MLOps is an abbreviation for "machine learning operations" and is about the development, deployment, and monitoring of AI. There are various tools to help with this. But having a strong organizational structure is also important.

- Even though a data scientist will help with testing AI models, it is usually a good idea to have a QA person. They can find those issues that may be missed but also help with non-technical problems, such as with the UI.

- Test-driven development is where you develop software by setting up tests to fail and then find ways to fix them. Essentially, it is a proactive approach in finding problems with the application.

- Monitoring of an AI system can be done with software tools. But there should still be ongoing tracking from data scientists and other employees. It's common for models to change over time and get less accurate.

- Security is another key part of the monitoring process since AI models use valuable data. This is why there should be coordination with IT.

- Adversarial machine learning is malware that destabilizes AI models.

- Periodically, the AI should be assessed for the ROI.

- In calculating ROI, the costs include factors like compensation for data scientists and other AI personnel, computer power/storage, consulting fees, data acquisition, maintenance and support, and tools.

- As for the "return" component of ROI, the most common is the reduction in the number of hours for a certain process. But there are certainly other benefits like improved customer experiences. AI may even result in higher revenues.

- For true adoption of AI, there needs to be change management. This involves techniques and strategies to galvanize an organization to take on a major effort. AI may be even more challenging with change management because there is often fear of the technology from employees.

Responsible AI

Ethics and transparency

In June 2020, IBM announced it would no longer offer facial recognition software. This came from CEO Arvind Krishna's letter to Congress. In it, he talked about how IBM had a long history of supporting civil rights, such as in terms of diversity with hiring and refusing to support Jim Crow laws.

As for the policy on facial recognition, Krishna noted: "IBM firmly opposes and will not condone uses of any technology, including facial recognition technology offered by other vendors, for mass surveillance, racial profiling, violations of basic human rights and freedoms, or any purpose which is not consistent with our values and Principles of Trust and Transparency. We believe now is the time to begin a national dialogue on whether and how facial recognition technology should be employed by domestic law enforcement agencies."[1]

This was not an indictment of AI, though. Instead, Krishna was making a call for the tech industry to have a shared responsibility to make sure that innovations were tested and audited for bias, especially in sensitive areas like law enforcement.

Krishna's letter had a swift impact. Other companies like Amazon and Microsoft announced changes to their own policies regarding facial recognition software.

---

[1]www.ibm.com/blogs/policy/facial-recognition-sunset-racial-justice-reforms/

© Tom Taulli 2021
T. Taulli, *Implementing AI Systems*, https://doi.org/10.1007/978-1-4842-6385-3_8

The move by IBM is part of a growing trend of responsible AI. It's about applying ethics, transparency, and explainability to the technology to avoid discrimination and unfairness.

In this chapter, we'll take a closer look at this and see how it can be a part of the AI process.

Importance of Responsible AI

When Amazon developed an AI-driven system to help improve the recruiting of employees, the company was enthused. This would be a great way to streamline a manual process but also get better results. Amazon used the technology from 2012 to 2014.

But there was a problem: The system mostly recommended white males! Amazon made multiple attempts to fix this glaring issue but they never worked. The company eventually abandoned the system.[2]

What happened? It was about the data. Keep in mind that, during the past, Amazon had generally hired males.

This example illustrates that responsible AI is usually not about data scientists who have ill intentions. Rather, the bias is often the result of data issues. And yes, data does reflect society's prejudices.

The AI was not necessarily wrong either. It was just looking at patterns and coming up with some predictions. But regardless, the ultimate impact was that many people lost out on getting a job at Amazon.

Bias in AI is often called a "silent killer" because it can be unnoticeable. Let's face it: Traditional accuracy metrics are mostly about finding patterns, not determining if a model is unfair or discriminatory. It also does not help that the data science community is not particularly diverse. Nor are IT departments. The upshot is that AI models can be flawed.

The good news is that responsible AI is becoming a higher priority item, especially as companies like IBM, Microsoft, and Amazon take public stands on this. Then again, as AI becomes more critical in our daily lives, there needs to be a focus on making sure the technology does not infringe on people's rights.

---

[2]www.reuters.com/article/us-amazon-com-jobs-automation-insight/amazon-scraps-secret-ai-recruiting-tool-that-showed-bias-against-women-idUSKCN1MK08G

Executive Buy-In

Senior executives may not have much visibility into their internal AI projects (this is especially the case for non-tech companies). But this could be a huge risk. If the AI goes awry, the company could be in jeopardy of being the target of backlash from the public. Or, in some cases, there may be scrutiny from regulators. The result could be damaging to the company's brand.

In light of this, the focus on responsible AI needs to be a priority for senior executives. They need to understand the potential risks of the technology and to set forth initiatives to mitigate these risks. The lead for this may actually not be the CTO or CIO. It may instead be from the general counsel and the chief of HR. After all, AI is likely to be the subject of more regulations in the years ahead.

The buy-in from senior management also should not just be rhetorical. There needs to be an effort that is backed up with real resources, such as in terms of training and hiring. Consider that consulting firms are also developing their own practices to help build responsible AI frameworks.

Interestingly enough, some companies have even set up a senior executive position for responsible AI. Usually this position is called the Chief AI Responsibility Officer.

Best Practices

Responsible AI is still very much in the nascent stages. For the most part, it has been the larger companies that have been setting up policies and procedures for this. But there are still few standards. This should be no surprise. Topics like ethics can be amorphous and different based on people's backgrounds and cultures. This is why the development of responsible AI policies can take time to truly implement and the process can be quite contentious.

Yet some important principles and best practices are emerging. So let's take a look at some of them.

Questioning

The AI team needs to periodically ask tough questions about the consequences of the application. What can go wrong? How might the technology be misused? What might we be missing? Is the data reflective of the population?

This questioning needs to be ingrained. There also needs to be an environment where criticism is encouraged. By doing this, there will likely be much progress in dealing with the potential risks of AI.

Something else: The ethical standards of the company, such as that part of HR and the legal department, should be a part of AI too. Often this means acting with honesty, integrity, loyalty, fairness, and respect.

Testing

As covered in this book, testing is a critical factor for successful AI. But the testing should be more than just finding errors and problems with the UI. There should also be an evaluation of the inherent problems with bias. The data scientists and QA people can definitely help. But it is a good idea to have others in the organization provide feedback.

Principles

It is recommended to create a set of responsible AI principles. Again, a good place to start is with the company's existing guidelines and approaches. But since AI has unique capabilities and risks, there should be other elements added. In this chapter, we'll take a look at how Microsoft approached this scenario.

Your responsible AI principles need to be in writing and periodically reviewed. What's more, you should establish an AI ethics board. The goal is to have a diverse team that can bring different viewpoints to the process.

Transparency

Transparency is paramount. AI can easily lead to fear and distrust for employees and customers. So with an AI project, there needs to be as much disclosure as possible about the goals, progress, and intentions.

Another good policy is to have an audit of the project, such as by a third party. In fact, this may be required by a regulatory agency. But even if not, an audit will provide an extra layer of guardrails but also allow for more transparency.

Vendors

In the evaluation of AI software, ask the vendor about whether there are systems that help with responsible AI. Are there metrics to gauge the bias in data? What about the compliance with the various regulations? Is the technology built to implement your company's own rules?

In-House Tools

Some companies are developing their own tools to improve responsible AI. Take the example of Getty Images, which is one of the largest suppliers of stock images, videos, and music assets.

Given the huge scale, the company needs automation systems to detect bias. To this end, Getty Images built a tool that calculates the proportion of ages, genders, and ethnicities for its digital assets. Thus, if the company is working on an AI project, and the training set is 70% male, then the data scientists will rebalance it.

Explainability

Deep learning AI models often are black boxes, which means it is not clear how the results are generated. For certain industries like finance and healthcare, this could mean that the technology would not meet regulatory requirements.

As a result, a major area for AI research is on explainability. And while there has definitely been progress, there is much to be done. But there are some companies, like Fiddler Labs, that provide solutions to help companies with their models.

However, in terms of AI projects, explainability is often overlooked. According to a survey from McKinsey & Co., about 39% of respondents understand the risks but only 21% were actively addressing them.[3]

Bounties

An effective technique to combat cybersecurity breaches is to pay bounties. That is, if a person identifies an inherent risk with a system, they will get a payment. Note that Google has paid $21 million in bounties.

But might this be used for responsible AI? Definitely. Actually, according to a paper from Google Brain, Intel, OpenAI, and other leading research labs, this was a key recommendation.[4]

---

[3]www.mckinsey.com/featured-insights/artificial-intelligence/global-ai-survey-ai-proves-its-worth-but-few-scale-impact
[4]https://venturebeat.com/2020/04/17/ai-researchers-propose-bias-bounties-to-put-ethics-principles-into-practice/

Responsible AI Case: Microsoft

In Chapter 1, we saw the terrible experience with Microsoft's chatbot, Tay. Within minutes, the chatbot was spouting racist and sexist messages! The main problem was that users were gaming the system. But regardless of the reasons, Microsoft had an escalating PR problem on its hands and had little choice but to shut down Tay within 24 hours.

After this, Microsoft did take concerted actions to improve its efforts with responsible AI. For the most part, the company is now one of the leaders in this category.

To this end, Microsoft has put together a set of ethical principles, which have been emulated by various other companies. Here's what they include:[5]

- **Fairness**: AI systems should treat all people fairly.
- **Reliability and Safety**: AI systems should perform reliably and safely.
- **Privacy and Security**: AI systems should be secure and respect privacy.
- **Inclusiveness**: AI systems should empower everyone and engage people.
- **Transparency**: AI systems should be understandable.
- **Accountability**: People should be accountable for AI systems.

Next, the company created an organization whose focus is on operationalizing the principles. This includes two parts:

- **Microsoft's AI and Ethics in Engineering and Research (AETHER) Committee**: This group provides recommendations about responsible AI. There are also working groups that engage in research and provide advice.
- **Office of Responsible AI (ORA)**: This group works to implement the core principles of responsible AI. It also helps promote public policies.

---

[5]www.microsoft.com/en-us/ai/responsible-ai?activetab=pivot1%3aprimaryr6

Conclusion

As you've seen in this book, AI has much potential for making major improvements. It truly is a transformative technology. And the innovation continues to move at a rapid pace.

But there is certainly a dark side to AI as well. Even top data scientists can make mistakes and develop systems that result in bias. This is why it is imperative for companies to put in place strategies for responsible AI—and this should start sooner than later.

So now we're ready for the last chapter in this book, where we will take a look at the future of AI.

Key Takeaways

- Responsible AI is about applying ethics, transparency, and explainability to the technology to avoid discrimination and unfairness. This part of the AI world is getting much more critical because of the pervasiveness of the technology.

- Bias in AI models is usually not intentional. Instead, it is often about data sets that are inadequate.

- It's essential to get executive buy-in for responsible AI. This also needs to involve a commitment of resources, such as with hiring and training. In some cases, a company will even create a new executive position for responsible AI.

- While responsible AI is still an emerging area, there are some important principles and best practices to keep in mind, such as the constant questioning of models; getting broad feedback on the models from across the organization; establishing a set of core principles (looking at your company's existing ethics frameworks can be a good place to start); having transparency with the goals of the AI; and focusing on explainability of the models.

- The executives that can be very helpful with responsible AI are the chief counsel and head of HR. These officers have extensive backgrounds in corporate ethics.

- Deep learning models are often considered black boxes, which means it is difficult to understand their underlying meaning. This could actually make it difficult to get approval from regulators. As a result, there has been more research on the explainability of AI.

Future of AI

Expect the growth to continue for the long-term.

A well-known optimist on AI is Ray Kurzweil. He is an inventor, such as of innovations in OCR (optical character recognition) and NLP (natural language processing). He has also written various books on topics like futurism and healthcare. Since 2012, Kurzweil has served as a director of engineering at Google.

So what are his predictions about AI? Well, he has noted: "Artificial intelligence will reach human levels by around 2029. Follow that out further to, say, 2045, we will have multiplied the intelligence, the human biological machine intelligence of our civilization a billion-fold."[1]

But of course, when it comes to predictions, especially those about technology, the failure rate is very high! So it should be no surprise that there are many AI pessimists as well.

One of the most famous was the late physicist and professor Stephen Hawking. In an interview with the BBC, he said, "The development of full artificial intelligence could spell the end of the human race."[2]

---

[1] https://dzone.com/articles/top-10-artificial-intelligence-quotes-that-will-in
[2] www.bbc.com/news/technology-30290540#:~:text=Prof%20Stephen%20
Hawking%2C%20one%20of,end%20of%20the%20human%20race.%22

© Tom Taulli 2021
T. Taulli, *Implementing AI Systems*, https://doi.org/10.1007/978-1-4842-6385-3_9

Such optimism vs. pessimism debates are definitely enlightening and helpful. It's a way to think through the consequences of AI.

But regardless, there is something that seems certain: that is, the technology will continue to grow rapidly and significantly impact the world. So in this chapter, we'll take a look at some of the major trends with AI.

5G

5G stands for the fifth generation of the mobile network. This version, though, will perhaps be the most transformative, as it will allow for much higher speeds, reliability, and capacity but also the seamless connectivity across machines and devices.

According to research from Qualcomm, 5G is forecasted to increase the worth of goods and services by $13.2 trillion by 2035 and there may be the creation of 22.3 million new jobs.[3]

But 5G will also likely be a game changer for AI. Because of the high speeds, it will be possible to handle much more of the analytics processing in the cloud. This will go a long way to increasing the power of AI models in the real world.

For example, there will be much more innovation of IoT (Internet of Things). The AI will be connected across complex global supply chains to improve efficiencies and predictions, such as for demand. This may be enhanced even with things like AI-connected refrigerators that can help with understanding usage patterns. But there are some other interesting applications like remote surgery, faster drug discovery, and autonomous cars.

Let's look at an interesting use case: Neteera. The founder, Isaac Litman, is a top entrepreneur, who was the CEO of Mobileye (a pioneer of automobile safety systems). In 2017, he sold the company to Intel for $15.3 billion and it became the centerpiece of the chip giant's self-driving efforts.

As for Neteera, it is the developer of AI systems that can detect very small movements in a person's skin, and this can be done without making any contact. This means minimizing the risk of contamination but also allowing for a much wider use of the technology, say in cars or homes.

The result is, by having a high-speed mobile approach, people can have easy access to medical diagnoses. But there are also potential treatments for sleep apnea detection and SIDS prevention for babies, just to name a few.

---

[3]www.qualcomm.com/invention/5g/what-is-5g

Regulation

At the Davos conference in early 2020, Alphabet CEO Sundar Pichai made some headlines when he said: "There is no question in my mind that artificial intelligence needs to be regulated. The question is how best to approach this."[4]

He would go on to propose "sensible regulation." But for the most part, he was vague on what this would entail.

Yet it was a clear-cut sign that he realized that government regulation would likely get more onerous. And he was not alone among the mega tech operators. The CEOs of Microsoft and Facebook have also indicated their willingness for more regulation.

But of course, their opinions involve much hedging. For example, in the case of Pichai, he does not want regulation that would stifle innovation.

It's important to keep in mind that there are emerging laws, such as for privacy, that are already impacting the development of AI. Examples include General Data Protection Regulation (GDPR), which is the framework for the European Union, and the California Consumer Privacy Act (CCPA).

In fact, some companies are even putting risk factors for AI regulation in their SEC filings. Here's an example from Lemonade: "State and federal lawmakers, and insurance regulators are focusing upon the use of AI broadly, including concerns about transparency, deception, and fairness in particular. Changes in laws or regulations, or changes in the interpretation of laws or regulations by a regulatory authority, specific to the use of AI, may decrease our revenues and earnings and may require us to change the manner in which we conduct some aspects of our business. In addition, our business and operations are subject to various U.S. federal, state, and local consumer protection laws, including laws which place restrictions on the use of automated tools and technologies to communicate with wireless telephone subscribers or consumers generally."[5]

In other words, it seems inevitable that there will be more regulation of AI, and businesses will need to find ways to navigate this.

---

[4] www.wsj.com/articles/tech-giants-new-appeal-to-governments-please-regulate-us-11580126502?mod=hp_lead_pos13
[5] www.sec.gov/Archives/edgar/data/1691421/000104746920003943/a2242013z424b4.htm#de40510_regulation

Quantum Computing

Moore's Law, which states that the number of transistors on a microchip doubles about every two years, has been a main driver for growth and innovation. But the prospects of this concept appear to be in danger.

At the 2019 CES event, Nvidia CEO and co-founder Jensen Huang said, "Moore's Law isn't possible anymore."[6] That is, traditional chip technologies are running into diminishing returns. This is particularly troublesome for AI since it relies heavily on high-end computer systems.

Granted, Jensen believes that his company's GPU technology is the future, and he is probably right. This approach has proven quite powerful.

But there are other innovations. And perhaps the most important is quantum computing. It's a category that has become a priority of the world's largest tech companies like Microsoft, Alibaba, IBM, and Google.

Quantum computing is based on the complex physics of subatomic particles. Instead of relying on 0s and 1s (bits) for computations, there are blended values from 0 to 1 (called quibits). This is essentially about handling probabilities and working in parallel. To pull this off, there is a need for such things as cryogenics and superconductivity.

This does seem like something straight out of science fiction. But keep in mind that quantum computing is still in the experimental phase and commercialization is not likely until the next few years. There is still much that needs to be worked out.

Yet the potential benefits of the technology are transformative. Quantum computing systems will be able to process enormous amounts of data at high speeds. All in all, it will make it easier to create advanced AI.

"Don't try to beat classical computers at ML/AI problems that classical computers are good at because they are really good at them," said David Hayes, who is the Head of Honeywell's Quantum Theory team. "Quantum computers are better suited for ML/AI problems that are still hard for classical computers like modeling complex probability distributions, or generative model problems."[7]

---

[6]www.cnet.com/news/moores-law-is-dead-nvidias-ceo-jensen-huang-says-at-ces-2019/
[7]From the author's interview with David Hayes on July 28, 2020.

What Does Hinton Think?

In Chapter 2, we learned about Geoffrey Hinton, who pioneered major breakthroughs in AI, such as with backpropagation. His theories ultimately led to the creation of deep learning.

Hinton's background is definitely interesting and inspirational. Even when he was a teenager in the 1950s he wanted to be a professor and study AI! Then again, his mom would say to him, "Be an academic or be a failure."[8]

When Hinton attended the University of Edinburgh for his PhD, the timing was terrible since it was a dark period of the first AI Winter. But this was no concern for him. He was convinced that neural networks would provide a great way to advance AI, and so he continued his work confidently. True, many people thought he was wasting his time. The perception was that AI was mostly a fringe topic. But hey, Hinton liked being a rebel and was willing to take the long view of things. He knew that computer power would eventually make it possible to show the true value of neural networks.

And yes, he was eventually vindicated. He is now called the "Godfather of Deep Learning" and won the Turing Award in 2018, along with Yoshua Bengio and Yann LeCun.

So whenever Hinton talks about AI, people listen.

So what is his view of the future? What are some of his takeaways about AI? Well, here are some quotes:

- "No, there's not going to be an AI winter, because it drives your cellphone. In the old AI winters, AI wasn't actually part of your everyday life. Now it is."[9]

- "I think things like reasoning, abstract reasoning, they're the kind of last things we learn to do, and I think they'll be among the last things these neural nets learn to do... Well, we are neural nets. Anything we can do they can do."[10]

- "Instead of programming them [computers], we now show them, and they figure it out. That's a completely different way of using computers, and computer science departments are built around the idea of programming computers. And they don't understand that sort of this showing computers is going to be as big as programming computers. Except they don't understand that half the

[8]https://torontolife.com/tech/ai-superstars-google-facebook-apple-studied-guy/
[9]www.wired.com/story/googles-ai-guru-computers-think-more-like-brains/
[10]www.wired.com/story/ai-pioneer-explains-evolution-neural-networks/

people in the department should be people who get computers to do things by showing them."[11]

- "If you can dramatically increase productivity and make more goodies to go around, that should be a good thing. Whether or not it turns out to be a good thing depends entirely on the social system, and doesn't depend at all on the technology. People are looking at the technology as if the technological advances are a problem. The problem is in the social systems, and whether we're going to have a social system that shares fairly, or one that focuses all the improvement on the 1% and treats the rest of the people like dirt. That's nothing to do with technology."[12]

Conclusion

We have come to the end of the book. And we've covered quite a bit. We looked at the fundamentals of AI and the various steps in the process for a successful implementation.

Granted, on your own AI journey, there will certainly be many tough challenges and complex issues. The technology is still evolving. So in your journey, the key is to always learn new ideas and approaches.

AI is also a team sport. There must be much collaboration to make an AI project that gets results. It's absolutely critical.

So then, good luck on your own journey. By reading this book, you will have a set of tools to get off to a great start!

Key Takeaways

- Predicting the trends for AI is quite difficult, if not impossible. Even the greatest minds in the industry have widely differing views. But there seems to be one thing that is certain: the growth will continue for the long haul. And the technology will increasingly become essential for business success.

- 5G stands for the fifth generation of the mobile network, which will mean much higher speeds. Because of this, the

---

[11]https://medium.com/@imior/interview-of-geoffrey-hinton-80c48a939282
[12]https://gizmodo.com/the-godfather-of-deep-learning-on-why-we-need-to-ensure-1831239688

technology will likely have a major impact on AI. This will be especially the case since more processing can be done in the cloud. Some of the applications include remote surgery, faster drug discovery, autonomous cars, and the Internet of Things.

- Regulation is likely to increase for AI. It is far from clear how this will play out. But large tech companies like Google, Facebook, IBM, and Microsoft have set forth proactive strategies to allow for reasonable protections while also finding ways to not damper innovation.

- Quantum computing is a radical new approach for developing machines. Instead of using 0s and 1s, there is a blend from 0 to 1, and the numbers vary based on probabilities. While quantum computing will take time to get to commercialization, the technology does have the potential of providing much more powerful AI models.

Glossary

Activation function: Used in deep learning models to help calculate non-linear relationships

Actuators: Electro-mechanical devices like motors. They help with the movement of a robot.

AI: See Artificial Intelligence

AI Winter: A prolonged period of time, such as in the 1970s and 1980s, when the AI industry came under much pressure, such as with cutbacks in funding

Artificial Intelligence: Where computers are able to learn from experience, which often involves processing data using sophisticated algorithms. Artificial intelligence is a broad category, which includes subsets like machine learning, deep learning, and natural language processing (NLP).

Artificial neural network (ANN): The most basic structure for a deep learning model. The ANN includes multiple hidden layers that process data through the use of sophisticated algorithms.

Automated machine learning (AutoML): A digital tool or platform that allows beginners to create their own AI models

Backpropagation: A major breakthrough in deep learning. Backpropagation allows for more efficient assigning of weightings in models.

© Tom Taulli 2021
T. Taulli, *Implementing AI Systems*, https://doi.org/10.1007/978-1-4842-6385-3

Bayes' theorem: A statistical measure used in machine learning that helps to provide a more accurate view of the probabilities

Big data: A category of technology that involves processing huge amounts of data. Big data is often described as having the three Vs—that is, volume, variety, and velocity.

Binning: Involves organizing data into groups

Categorical data: Data that does not have a numerical meaning but instead has textual meaning, say with describing race or gender

Cerebral cortex: Part of the human brain that has the most similarities to AI. It helps with thinking and other cognitive activities

Chatbot: An AI system that communicates with people

Clustering: A form of unsupervised learning that takes unlabeled data and uses algorithms to put similar items into groups

Convolutional neural network (CNN): A deep learning model that goes through different variations—or convolutions—of analysis on data. CNNs are often used for complex applications like facial recognition.

Data lake: Allows for the storage and processing of massive amounts of structured and unstructured data. There is often little to no need to reformat the data.

Data type: The kind of information a variable represents, such as a Boolean, integer, string, or floating point number

Decision tree: A machine learning algorithm that is a workflow of decision paths

Deepfake: Involves using deep learning models to create images or videos that are misleading or harmful

Deep learning: A type of AI that uses neural networks, which mimic the processes of the brain. Much of the innovation in the field during the past decade has been with deep learning research.

Ensemble modelling: Involves using more than one model for generating predictions

ETL (extraction, transformation, and load): A form of data integration that is typically used in a data warehouse

Ethics Board: A committee that evaluates the issues of AI projects

Expert system: An early type of an AI application that emerged in the 1980s. It used sophisticated logic systems to help understand certain areas like medicine, finance, and manufacturing.

Explainability: The process of understanding the underlying causes of a deep learning model

False positive: When a model prediction shows that the result is true even though it is not.

Feature: This is a column of data.

Feature engineering: See Feature extraction

Feature extraction: Describes the process of selecting the variables for an AI model

Feed-forward neural network: A deep learning model that processes data in a linear direction through the hidden layers. There is no cycling back.

Generative adversarial network (GAN): Developed by AI researcher Ian Goodfellow, this is a next-generation deep learning model that helps to create new outputs like audio, text, or video.

GPUs (graphics processing units): Chips that were originally used for high-speed video games because of their ability to process large amounts of data quickly. But GPUs have also proven to be adept at handling AI applications.

Hadoop: Allows for managing big data, such as by making it possible to create sophisticated data warehouses

Hidden layers: The different levels of analysis in a deep learning model

Hidden Markov model (HMM): An algorithm that is used to decipher spoken words

Hyperparameters: Features in a model that cannot be learned directly from the training process

Instance: This is a row of data.

Jupyter notebook: A web-based app that makes it easy to code in Python and R to create visualizations and import AI systems

K-means clustering: An algorithm that is effective for grouping similar unlabeled data

K-nearest neighbor (k-NN): A machine learning algorithm that classifies data based on similarities

Lemmatization: A process in NLP that removes affixes or prefixes so as to focus on finding similar root words

Lidar (light detection and ranging): A device—which is usually at the top of an autonomous car—that shoots laser beams to measure the surroundings

Linear regression: Shows the relationship between certain variables, which can help with predictions for machine learning systems

Machine learning: Where a computer can learn and improve by processing data without having to be explicitly programmed. Machine learning is a subset of AI.

Metadata: This is data about data—that is, descriptions. For example, a music file can have metadata like the size, length, date of upload, comments, genre, artist, and so on.

Naïve Bayes classifier: A method of machine learning that uses Bayes' theorem to make predictions, but the variables are independent from each other.

Named entity recognition: In the NLP process, this involves identifying words that represent locations, persons, and organizations.

Natural language processing (NLP): A subset of AI that deals with how computers understand and manipulate language

Neural network: A sophisticated AI model that mimics the brain. A neural network has various layers that attempt to find unique patterns that involve multiple layers of analysis.

Normal distribution: A plot of data that looks like a bell and the midpoint is the mean.

NoSQL system: A next-generation database. The information is based on a document model so as to allow for more flexibility with analysis as well as the handling of structured and unstructured data.

Ordinal data: A mix of numerical and categorical data, such as an Amazon.com rating for a product

Overfitting: Where a model is not accurate because the data is not reflective of what is being tested or there is a focus on the wrong features

Pearson correlation: Shows the strength of a correlation—from 1 to -1. The closer it is to 1, the more accurate the correlation.

Predictive analytics: Involves using data to make forecasts

Python: A computer language that has become the standard in developing AI models

PyTorch: A platform, developed by Facebook, that allows for the creation of sophisticated AI models

Recurrent neural network (RNN): A deep learning model that processes prior inputs across time. A common use case is when a person types in characters in a messaging app and the AI predicts the next word.

Reinforcement learning: An approach to creating an AI model where the system is rewarded for the right predictions and punished for the wrong ones.

Relational database: A database, whose roots go back to the 1970s, that creates relationships among tables of data and has a scripting language called SQL

R-squared: Provides a way to gauge the accuracy of a regression. An R-squared ranges from 0 to 1. And the closer a model is to 1, the higher the accuracy.

Sentiment analysis: This is where you mine social media data and find the trends.

Sensor: The typical sensor is a camera or a Lidar, which uses a laser scanner to create 3D images.

Sigmoid: A common activation function for a deep learning model. It has a value that ranges from 0 to 1. The closer it is to 1, the higher the accuracy.

Standard deviation: Measures the average distance from the mean, which gives a sense of the variation in the data

Stemming: Describes the process of reducing a word to its root (or lemma), such as by removing affixes and suffixes

Strong AI: This is true AI, in which a machine is able to engage in human-like abilities like open-ended discussions

Structured data: Data that is usually stored in a relational database or spreadsheet, as the information is in a preformatted structure (like Social Security numbers, addresses, and point of sale information).

Tagging parts of speech (POS): In the NLP process, this involves going through text and designating each word to its proper grammatical form, say nouns, verbs, adverbs, etc.

TensorFlow: An open source platform, backed by Google, that allows for the creation of sophisticated AI models

Test data: Data that a model's accuracy is evaluated upon

Training data: Data that is used to create an AI algorithm

True positive: When a model makes a correct prediction

Turing Test: Created by Alan Turing, this is a way to determine if a system has achieved true AI. The test involves a person who asks questions to two participants—one human, the other a computer. If it is not clear who is the human, then the Turing Test has been passed.

Unstructured data: Data that does not have predefined formatting, such as images, videos, and audio files

Supervised learning: An AI model that uses labeled data. This is the most common approach.

Unsupervised learning: Involves an AI model that uses unlabeled data. Generally, this involves a deep learning systems to detect patterns.

Vanishing gradient problem: Explains how the accuracy decays as a deep learning model gets larger

Virtual assistant: An AI device that helps people with their daily activities

Weak AI: This is where AI is used for a particular use case, such as with Apple's Siri

Index

© Tom Taulli 2021
T. Taulli, *Implementing AI Systems*, https://doi.org/10.1007/978-1-4842-6385-3